CHANGING TIMES
Religion and Society in Nineteenth-Century Celbridge

Maynooth Studies in Local History

GENERAL EDITOR Raymond Gillespie

This is one of the new pamphlets published in 1997 in the Maynooth Studies in Local History series. Like earlier titles in the series, published in 1995 and 1996, each study is derived from a thesis completed in connection with the Maynooth M.A. course in local history.

The localities studied are defined not by administrative boundaries but by the nature of the community bonds which shaped people's experiences in the past, both holding them together and driving them apart. Ranging across family, village, parish, town, and estate, the pamphlets investigate how people in these varied communities lived out their lives and responded to changes in the outside world.

These Maynooth Studies in Local History explore the richness and diversity of the Irish historical experience, and in doing so present local history as the vibrant and challenging discipline that it is.

Maynooth Studies in Local History: Number 10

Changing Times

Religion and Society in Nineteenth-Century Celbridge

Desmond J. O'Dowd

IRISH ACADEMIC PRESS

Set in 10 on 12 point Bembo by
Carrigboy Typesetting Services, Co. Cork
and published by
IRISH ACADEMIC PRESS LTD
Northumberland House
44, Northumberland Road, Ballsbridge, Dublin 4, Ireland
and in North America by
IRISH ACADEMIC PRESS LTD
c/o ISBS, 5804 NE Hassalo Street, Portland, OR 97123

A catalogue record for this title
is available from the British Library.

ISBN 0-7165-2635-2

Printed in Ireland
by ColourBooks, Dublin

Contents

Preface

I wish to acknowledge with gratitude some of the many people who encouraged and assisted me to complete this work, and to whom no blame is attached for its weaknesses and inaccuracies.

I am indebted to the parish priest of Celbridge Father Carmody and to the Church of Ireland rector, David Boylan, for their co-operation in my research: to Professor R.V. Comerford who as my supervisor gave me invaluable advice and assistance: to Dr. Raymond Gillespie whose course has been an inspiration and a pleasure: to Gráinne Feeney for patient and cheerful typing: to Kate, Ben and Cian who endured much, and above all to Patricia who endured most and to whom this work is dedicated.

Introduction

Celbridge today is a town of 12,000 people, located on the banks of the River Liffey, twelve miles west of the city of Dublin. It has one long and wide street which stretches from the gates of Castletown House to the narrow bridge which was and is the principal point of entry to the town. On Sunday mornings this street is usually thronged with people making their way to and from church. Religion is today, as it was in the past, an important aspect in the life of the village and its people. Religion would not be seen today as a source of division either politically or socially. The schools however remain denominational. I hope in my study of religion in nineteenth century Celbridge to come to a greater understanding of the town and its people as they were then. In learning more about the town in its past, I hope to understand more of what it has become today.

To understand why I intend to focus on religion, let me first put together a picture of the parish as it was at the beginning of the nineteenth century. Though there was certainly human habitation in the area dating back to the early Christian era, when Saint Mochua is reputed to have built a monastery beside the river, the town's present appearance was only realised in the eighteenth century. William 'Speaker' Conolly, reputed at the time to be Ireland's richest man, acquired property in the area in 1709.[1] Conolly had acquired great wealth in the purchase and re-sale of forfeited estates after the battle of the Boyne in 1690. Following his election as member of Parliament for Donegal in 1715 he was appointed Speaker of the Irish House of Commons and so acquired his nickname. In 1722 work began on the construction of Castletown House for Conolly – the largest and finest Palladian country house in Ireland. People with money to invest followed Conolly to Kildrought. Robert Ballie, a prosperous Dublin upholsterer came in 1720 and built Kildrought House. George Finey, Conolly's agent also contributed to the new development of the town.[2] Castletown brought many visitors from afar to the area. Charles Tophan Bowden who visited the house in 1790 described it as 'vastly superior to anything I have seen in England'.[3] Twiss who also visited Castletown said that 'it is the only house in Ireland to which the term palace may be applied'.[4] The *New Traveller's Guide* published in 1819 gives a good picture of what the town would have looked like – 'on the right bank of the Liffey is situated the town of Celbridge. There is a fine stone bridge thrown over the Liffey: at the lower extremity of the town an elegant church has been lately erected in an angle of the Castletown demesne on the bank of the river: its lofty square

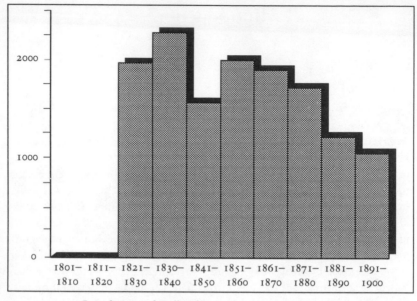

1. Population of Celbridge in the nineteenth century

steeple and spire form a delightful termination to the end of a long street'.[5]
Such was the excellent quality of farmland in the area and also presumably because of its proximity to Dublin there was, as the *Post Chaise Companion* de-
scribes, as 'many handsome seats in the area'.[6] The ordinary people of the area
are described by Frenchman Coquebert de Montbret, who was a visitor in the
1790s, as 'poorly clad, English speaking peasants'.[7] Another famous visitor to
the area, Arthur Young, does give us an inkling as to the existence of the less
well off when he states that 'turnips were sown in the fields up to 30 years ago
but left off on account of the poor stealing them'.[8]

The town's mainly agricultural based economy was to change however
when Lawrence Atkinson entered into partnership with Thomas and Jeremiah
Haughton of Huddersfield and they took control of the old corn and tuck
mills located beside the Liffey bridge in 1808.[9] Edward Wakefield inspected
the factory in 1809 and his reports are of interest – 'They import much of
their wool from England and purchase it in the fleece ... all of this is per-
formed by machinery and children, with the assistance of a few women who
attend them. The children earn from 3s 6d to 4s a week ... The working day
consists of thirteen hours out of which the people employed are allowed half
an hour for breakfast and an hour for dinner'.[10]

Perhaps because of the relatively good local employment situation,
Celbridge seems to have come through the turmoils of the 1798 rebellion un-
scathed. The rebellion papers contain a list of rebels who marched into
Celbridge in arms during the rebellion.[11] However of the 320 people who

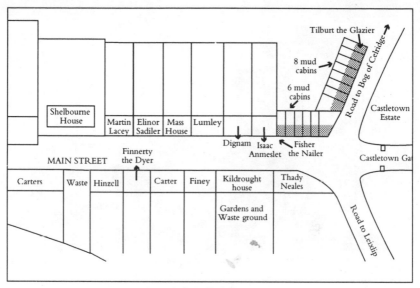

2. Map of Celbridge 1700–1726

claimed to have suffered loss in the Kildare area during the rebellion only one
claim came from Celbridge – and that loss was actually sustained on the road
and not in Celbridge.[12] The rebellion, according to Lena Boylan, was not re-
stricted to one social group, as the Conolly family for example had relatives
on both sides.[13] Political power lay completely in the hands of a small
Protestant elite. As late as 1840, after Catholic Emancipation, whereas the population of the country was 108,424 the number of people entitled to vote was
1,152.[14] Local government such as it was, consisted of grand juries and here
again these were composed entirely of members of the Established Church
who were also people of property.

According to the maps of the time, such as Taylor and Skinner published
in 1778, Celbridge is located on the Dublin to Portarlington road.[15] While
this would indicate that Portarlington was a town of greater economic importance than it is today, it also indicates a large amount of road traffic car-
rying turf from the environs of Portarlington which travelled via Celbridge to
the city of Dublin. Alex Taylor's map of the county of Kildare published in
1783 again depicts the town of Celbridge on the level area of land to the
north-east of the pronounced and clearly identified Bog of Allen.[16] It is also
certain that large amounts of hay and straw for horses would have been trans-
ported through the town on its way to Dublin. There are many stories told
by local people regarding the herds of cattle which were driven through the
town on their way to the markets of Dublin.

The first official census figures for the parish of Celbridge (Fig 1) show a
population of 1,949 in 1821.[17] Considering the mills were undergoing ex-

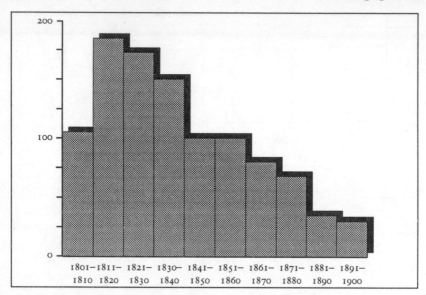

3. Church of Ireland Baptisms – Parish of Celbridge, 1800–1900

pansion at this time we may presume that the figure for the start of the century would have been somewhat less than that.

There is evidence from local maps (Fig 2) of a Catholic Mass House having been located as it is today in the very centre of the main street and this property was provided rent free by the Conolly family. Parish priest Henry Murphy was in 1890 able to trace back an unbroken line of previous parish priests in the area to 1680.[18] All of this would give the impression that Catholicism was, at the very least, tolerated in the area. The Church of Ireland community was much smaller as can be seen from an analysis of their Baptism and Marriage Register Book (Figs 3, 4). Their church building was located since 1812 symbolically, just within the gates of Castletown demesne. The Royal Commission on Education's second report in 1826 records that there were eleven teaching centres in Celbridge at that time. Most of the education provided would seem to have been on a small scale and of denominational nature in some cases – six Catholics only, four mixed and Celbridge Charter school which had only Protestant girls at that time.[19]

So in any analysis of Celbridge at the beginning of the nineteenth century, religion would seem to have been an important factor in deciding a persons social status, occupation, education and even what they would likely aspire to. It is the key to understanding how and why the town operated. This is why I have chosen to use the excellent Church sources to study the development of religion in the nineteenth century. I am seeking the inside picture of this force which was shaping the history of the town. I want to compare what was happening on a national stage with what was happening in this small community.

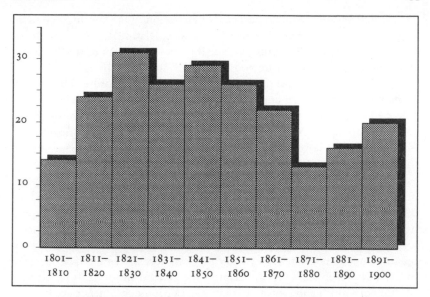

4. Church of Ireland marriages – Parish of Celbridge, 1800–1900

The Catholic Church nationally was working on expanding its profile and influence and to do this it needed a more sophisticated organisation. The Church of Ireland nationally had to begin to learn to stand on its own – free from the financial prop of tithes and its state prop of establishment.

I have deliberately concentrated my research on these two church groups alone as the number of people who were not adherents to these two main bodies were minimal – in 1871 only thirty-six out of a total parish population of 1,745.[20] I will devote the first two chapters to a separate study of the important issues confronted by each church, as can be seen from a study of their separate papers. In the third chapter I hope to examine the relationship between these two Christian churches – co-operation and conflict. I will also be searching always for the human stories of life in the parish.

The Roman Catholic parish and the Established parish are both known as 'United Parishes of Celbridge and Straffan'. I shall concentrate my study on the Celbridge section which was of greater importance and size than the small rural community of Straffan. The papers of the Catholic church consist principally of letters and parish reports which were sent from the parish to various archbishops of Dublin during the nineteenth century. This collection of six parish reports (covering the period 1820–1848) and forty five items of correspondence are all located in the Dublin Diocesan Archives. Many are of a personal and private nature. Within the parish itself are located the Baptism Registers from 1768 and the Marriage Registers from 1779. There is also a most interesting ledger book which gives in minute detail the receipts and expenditure on parochial buildings, including the erection of a new church, from

1855–1868. Because of the importance of education to the area of religion in any study, I have included material available relating to the schools in Celbridge – principally the papers of the Commissioners of the National Board of Education which are housed in the National Archives.

The Church of Ireland papers are of a more formal nature. There are a complete set of Baptism and Marriage Registers from 1777, Select Vestry Minute books from 1846 to 1860 and 1871 to 1882, Preachers' books from 1861 to 1905 and the Minute Books of the Young Men's Christian Association from 1862 to 1863. Again I shall supplement this material with papers from the education files of the National Archives.

Celbridge has not been overindulged by the local historian in the past. Tony Doohan has written a brief but well-informed *History of Celbridge*.[21] As this was intended primarily for the use of schools it has not investigated primary sources to any great degree. Lena Boylan has written numerous articles[22] for journals on various people and places in the history of the town. This is the first study to research any aspect of religious development in the town and to examine on its influence in shaping the general history of the locality. Monsignor Corish and Donal Harman Akenson, among others, have studied religious developments at this time on a national level. I hope that my study of religion in one small nineteenth-century community may in some way contribute to the understanding of the broader picture.

The Roman Catholic Church in Nineteenth-Century Celbridge

This chapter examines the organisation and structure of the Catholic church in the parish, its finances, its involvement in education and its expanding role in society.

The organisation of the parish of Celbridge in the nineteenth century depended upon and centred around the parish priest. Each priest would stamp his own identity on the parish for the period in which he held the position. During the nineteenth century ten men held the position of parish priest of Celbridge at different times.[1]

Years as Parish Priest of Celbridge	Name
1780–1802	Fr. James Boyce
1802–1820	Fr. Patrick Brennan
1821–1829	Fr. James Callan
1833–1855	Fr. Patrick O'Rourke
1855–1865	Fr. Daniel Byrne
1865–1873	Fr. Miles McManus
1873–1889	Fr. John Donovan
1889–1892	Fr. Henry Murphy
1892–1906	Fr. Francis Maguire

Many of these men left very little written material behind them and so it is difficult to assess their full role in the development of the parish. There is enough surviving information on Patrick O'Rourke, Daniel Byrne and Henry Murphy to merit comment on their role and personality and this I shall do at the conclusion of the chapter, having looked at their influence and role in the surviving papers and records pertaining to the Catholic church.

The earliest written records relating to the parish, apart from the baptism and marriage registers, are the six parish reports. These cover the years 1820, 1833, 1834, 1839, 1845, 1848. A parish report was compiled by the parish priest and dispatched to the archbishop prior to a visitation by the archbishop to the parish. They differ in the amount of data they contain and their accuracy as we shall see, can be open to question.

The parish of Celbridge is described in the 1820 parish report[2] by parish priest Patrick Brennan, 'your Grace's most devoted and humble servant, as having 320 houses of Catholics and 40 houses of Sectaries (non-Catholics)'. This is the only information supplied apart from the patron saints of the two churches in the parish – Celbridge dedicated to Saint Mochua and Straffan to Saint Patrick.

The second report[3] filed in 1833 by Rev. James Murphy provides a picture of a parish which he would like to present as organised and pious. 'There is a library for the chapel in Celbridge. There are 3 confraternities (prayer groups) and more than 200 monthly communicants. There are no people more attentive to their religious duties and particularly to the Christmas and Easter duties than those who are resident in this parish'. Here we have a church that has certainly left the penal days behind and has organised its faithful into devotional groups. Gone are the looser religious practices associated with the penal times when parishes often had no priest to minister regularly to them. Now there are monthly communicants and duties which imply obligation and also the opportunity to fulfil such duties. The laity are involved in the work of the parish: 'There is a Sunday school in the chapel of Celbridge in which upwards of 300 children are taught spelling, reading and Christian doctrine'. There is no mention of the number of priests in the parish but it does report that two masses were said each Sunday in Celbridge and one in Straffan. Priests were by church law[4] only allowed to say one mass per day in the same church and this would seem to imply that there was at least one curate in the parish though none appears in the *Catholic Directory* list of curates[5] for that time. Certainly the parish had need of at least one curate if we are to take as accurate the report of 1834[6] sent to the archbishop.

According to Fr. O'Rourke's figures there were 3,060 Catholics in Celbridge and 766 Catholics in Straffan. This out of a total population of 4,502. (These figures do not agree with the 1831 published state census figures which would put a total for the civil parish of Celbridge (this would exclude Straffan) at 2,295).[7]

The 1839 Parish Report[8] records no increase in the number of masses said. From this we must surmise that attendance at Sunday mass for all of the Catholic population was not at all expected or indeed feasible especially when one considers the small size of the chapel houses of the time – no drawing of Celbridge chapel house is available but drawings of nearby Leixlip and Maynooth are in existence.[9] There is emphasis on religious instruction – 'Catechism has been taught in both chapels during the last two years, every evening for two hours from the first of April until the first of October' – obviously making use of natural light in what would have been a dark badly-lit chapel house. This combined with 'a Sunday school in which better than 300 males and female are taught to read by voluntary teachers' would seem to emphasise the importance placed on education in the parish.

The 1845 Parish Report[10] is signed by Father O'Rourke, P.P. and also Patrick Woods, his curate. There was no lease or rent on the chapel or the attached chapel-house thanks to the generosity of the Conolly family. Though there was a chalice for both chapels there was only one ciborium (vessel for the communion breads) to be shared between the two, which might indicate a paucity of funds. Celbridge workhouse which opened in 1841 had also to be included – 'there is also a chalice for the workhouse and everything necessary for the decent decoration of the altar.'

The 1848 Report[11] is almost identical to all the previous reports in its description of Sunday schools, confraternities, masses and other religious ceremonies. This would indicate great continuity in the parish over the years and also a sustained effort at educating the young Catholics. Again Fr. O'Rourke seems to feel that his parish can be judged a success, from a religious practice perspective, because of the high numbers of parishioners who take Holy Communion – 'the number of monthly communicants is very considerable, more than 200'. By today's standards this would be considered a very small number out of a total population of more than 3,000 which shows a different attitude towards receiving Holy Communion than is common today.

The parish report supplied basic data to the archbishop which gave him an overview of the parish – its property, number of parishioners and facilities for worship and instruction. We must keep in mind that the Catholic church was a poor church serving poor people but after Catholic Emancipation in 1828 it was beginning to hold its head up. No doubt the visit of the archbishop reflected this new emergence from its hidden church image of the previous century – a time to celebrate and demonstrate the religious fervour of the parish. For the archbishop the report and the visit would help him assess the needs of the parish and also establish his control of it. The penal laws of the seventeenth and eighteenth century had often removed links in the Catholic church's hierarchical chain of command.

I feel however that all was not as well as these reports portray. These parish reports do give a clear picture of what the priests would like their parishes to be and we can expect that as they completed their parish reports, which would be presented to the archbishop before he visited the parish, they would want to be as positive as possible in their description. The 1833 Report drawn up by Fr. James Murphy was most firmly contradicted in a letter to the archbishop's secretary by a member of the nearby Maynooth college clergy in 1834.[12] 'The state of Celbridge is deplorable and must remain so unless an efficacious remedy is applied.' The remedy proposed was that 'Murphy [the parish priest] be induced to give up the parish on a pension and let O'Rourke [the curate] be named as Parish Priest.' The problems identified in the parish were 'no free Catholic schools, the non residence of the parish priest and the want of authority.' The tone of the letter was one of fear that if the present system continued much longer 'Catholicity I feel will decrease.' This letter if correct in is assertions would certainly contradict the picture painted by the parish reports of a church well organised. It betrays a feeling of insecurity on the part of the church and also of course is evidence of the ever-present human conflict in any organisation.

The organisation of the church depended upon the personnel and as the church became more institutionalised, financial provision had to be made for retiring priests. One year after the scathing letter of the previous paragraph was written, Fr. Murphy writes[13] to the archbishop as follows – 'I the undersigned Pastor of Celbridge, for many years engaged in the sacred ministry, worn out not by work but by ill-health and difficulties, commend, hand-over and resign my above mentioned parish, with all its right, references and obligations to the pastoral care of your Grace, that you may provide for it as best you can, according to your Holy Wisdom. For myself only (if your Grace and the Holy See shall see fit) that a sum in the amount of thirty pounds be deducted from the revenue to provide an annual pension.' That he was anxious that the parish would provide his yearly pension would indicate that specific arrangements had not been made prior to this, to cover the eventuality of early retirement. That an important point was at issue here was evident when the archbishop wrote[14] to the Pope Gregory XVI in Latin and which if translated is as follows – 'James Murphy already broken in strength, through indifferent health ... has resigned his parish freely ... in the hope however that he will receive some annual pension lest he should be reduced entirely to beggary.' Written at the bottom of this letter was the following – 'At an audience with the Holy Father held on the 5th July, 1835, our Supreme Lord, Gregory XVI, by Divine Providence Pope, ... graciously returned the petition to the judgement and prudence of the Reverend Father, the Lord Archbishop of Dublin.' Even at this early period of the century, the bureaucratic chain of command direct to Rome, was clearly identified but is it also interesting to note the almost legalistic terms used in the correspondence. Fr. Murphy would seem have been, as such, the legal owner of the parish with all its rights, revenues and obligations. The parish priest would seem to have been offering to trade these in return for his pension. It is impossible also not to feel sympathy for this exhausted old man, who it seems was almost reduced to pleading for provision to be made for his future.

Arrangements had also to be made by the developing church organisation for a fair recompense for any curates employed. The much praised Fr. O'Rourke (P.P. 1833 to 1855) himself came under severe criticism in a letter written by curate Fr. Lynch dated 2nd May 1854.[15] 'My complaint is this, not living with the P.P. [parish priest] I do not receive what I am entitled to – one third of all parochial revenues – by statutes of the Diocese.' An increasingly sophisticated church had to draw up what P.J. Corish calls 'a curates' charter.'[16] Henceforth the bishop had the right to name a curate and the curate had a legal right to a defined share of the parish revenue. That this charter was resented by Fr. O'Rourke can be seen in this same letter of his curate Fr. Lynch – 'In the first six months after I came here, out of collections made at Straffan chapel, I received only ten pence a week – the remaining portion the Parish Priest retained as his quota and for expenses, one of the items for which he debits me for, is the wear and tear of his horse and car and man.'[17]

Certainly this story tells us much about Fr. O'Rourke's financial practices which I will elaborate on further at the conclusion of the chapter. It also gives an insight into the harsh financial problems faced by these clergymen, as they tried to minister to their flock and sustain themselves at the same time. As well as these money worries, the priest had to contend with the expectation of a transfer out of his parish at the request of the archbishop.

The clergy's correspondence to the archbishop reveals a greater amount of interference by the archbishop in the life of the parish from the 1850s on. In many cases transfer of a priest from his parish was often unexpected and without any particular reason. The archbishop's actions were usually motivated by the desire to have his diocese run efficiently. This transfer of personnel did not always suit the individuals involved as can be seen in Daniel Byrne's (P.P. 1855 to 1865) letter dated 22 January 1863 in which he objects to the transfer of his curate Fr. Langan from the parish as 'he was admirably suited to the place and the place to him.'[18] The following year Fr. Byrne was to find it was himself who was being moved by the archbishop to a new parish in Rathfarnham. The same Fr. Byrne was a man of exceptional energy who certainly matched the challenges facing the church. 'I now resign into your Graces hands the charge of Celbridge parish which I have held for nine years. The two (new) churches are now complete, there are five schools in operation with an average attendance of 300 children. The parochial house is far advanced and I am happy to say that my successor will not only come in free from debt, but having something to his credit.'[19] The archbishop was probably already aware of Fr. Byrne's fund-raising and financial skills and wished to put them to good use outside of Celbridge now that the parish was in good order.

As the century passed more and more correspondence passed between parish and archbishop's house, on what would often seem to be trivial matters such as arrangements for a visit by the archbishop in 1880,[20] permission to have mass said in a private house in 1871,[21] and a request to have a mission in the parish.[22] Correspondence would have been swifter as the century progressed and we read in Samuel Lewis's *Topographical Dictionary*[23] for the village that there were already two delivery and dispatch times for mail by 1837. Much of this correspondence signifies a greater intrusion by the church authorities into what at the beginning of the century would have been areas under the more isolated authority of the parish priest. A January 1877 letter from Fr.

John Donovan P.P. requesting a mission in the parish is evidence that he felt he had a right to call on assistance from outside the parish in his quest to save the souls of his parishioners – 'The people here require and have a claim on one – it is twenty years since there was one here and many have fallen away from the practices of religion and there is no other chance of recalling these to feeling a sense of duty except through a mission.' Such was the attraction of the mission, with fire and brimstone preachers shaking the faithful out of their complacency, while at the same time adding a touch of drama and colour to their lives, that he said – 'We would have had it long since only we have no funds.'[24] The shortage of funds may have been related to the onset of decline in the local mills. But what is more obvious in his pleading letter, is his genuine fear that some of his flock were on the path to damnation and that he needed help to save them.

The parish registers contain in themselves many clues, as to the developing organisation of the church in Celbridge. The very existence of baptism registers dating from 1768 and marriage registers from 1769 indicate a church that had become increasingly institutionalised. The importance of keeping these records must have become more evident as the years went by, because the meticulous Henry Murphy P.P. in 1893 wrote – 'The oldest register belonging to the parish which I have found commences July 10 1768. The book was in bad condition, the paper beginning to flake, I have therefore commenced the following copy 24/4/1890.'[25] In the 1890s, the issue of boundaries between parishes, often a matter for disagreement, was like many other areas to be settled and the agreed boundaries reported to the archbishop. On the inside cover of a number of registers we have very detailed statements of the parish boundaries e.g. '29/10/1891 I brought the marked sheet of 6 inch ordinance survey maps to Kill and went over the marked boundaries of the above with Dr. Going P.P. and Fr. Delaney C.C. of Kill [an adjoining parish] who both agreed that the above [parish boundaries] were correct.'[26] Why the boundary issue was tackled in such great detail, including streams, fields, large rocks, etc, at this time is open to question. Was it to stop financial disputes between parishes regarding where and to whom certain people would pay their religious financial dues? Or is it another indication of increased bureaucracy? Analysis of the Registers also reveals much regarding the workload of the parish clergy. This increased workload in the middle decades of the century, coincided with the prospering of the mills and is reflected in the presence of two curates in the parish for the period 1854–1874 (See Appendix 1).

The total number of Roman Catholic baptisms registered for the period 1801 to 1900 was 7,968 and the total number of marriages registered for the same period was 1,512 (See Figures 5 and 6). The following extracts from the complete chart in Appendix 2 indicate the trends of the parish.

Registered Baptisms

1801 to 1810	705
1841 to 1850	1,004
1891 to 1900	523

As is clearly seen from Figure 5, there was a severe decline in baptisms registered after 1870 which can be related to the decline of the mills after 1870. It is worth noticing the high numbers registered through the years of 1841 to 1850 when there were 1,004 baptisms. This would confirm the belief that Celbridge remained relatively untouched by the famine. The disaster for Celbridge came at the end of the century when the mills had declined (1881 to 1890 – registered baptisms 505; 1891 to 1900 – registered baptisms 523).

A glance at the figures for registered marriages in the Catholic church reveals a similar story of decline at the century's end. This extract from Appendix 2 indicates the general trend.

1801 to 1810	109 Catholic Marriages
1841 to 1850	219 Catholic Marriages
1891 to 1900	84 Catholic Marriages

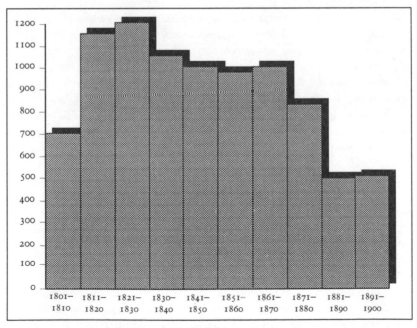

5. Roman Catholic Baptisms, 1800–1900

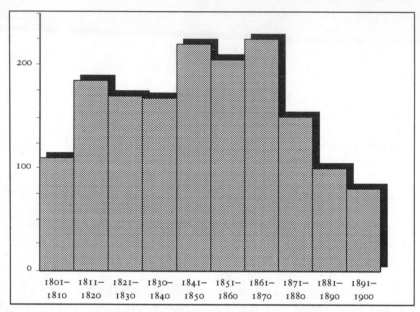

6. Roman Catholic Marriages, 1800–1900

From Fig 6 it is clear that the peak years for marriage were 1841 to 1870, a time when much of the rest of the country had its population decimated by famine, disease and emigration. These middle decades, when the need for marriages, baptisms and other religious ministries were at their highest, co-incide with the presence of two curates in the parish to aid the parish priest, (See Appendix 1). As will be shown in the section dealing with finances later, these were also the decades when the building of a bigger church (1859) and an elaborate house for the parish priest (1866) were also undertaken.

This brief look at the structure and organisation of the Catholic church in Celbridge revealed an organisation undergoing change. The demographic growth of the parish until the 1870s and then its sharp decline put pressure on the church to cope with its expanding congregation and then with the poverty and decline in the final decades. The church organisation was built around the parish priest with the support of his curate(s). These men had to struggle to maintain their own standard of living, worry about their future se-curity in the event of illness or old age and could expect to be transferred to another parish at any time. During this century the local church was losing much of its penal times autonomy to the archbishops of Dublin. There was an increase in the amount of outside interference and also a more organised ap-proach to the keeping of registers and the definition of parish boundaries. The brief parish reports covering the early decades talk paternally about the faith-ful being organised into devotional prayer groups (confraternities), being en-couraged to receive Holy Communion on a monthly basis and it would seem that every effort was made to teach the children the fundamentals of their faith, in the chapel house. It also seems evident that attending weekly mass in the chapel house was neither feasible nor expected of all of the parishioners. In some of the papers looked at there seems to be a tremendous insecurity that the faithful will be lost to the devil or to Protestantism. The sections which follow on the church's expanding secular role, its finances and involvement in education, I hope will add to the clarity of the hazy picture already drawn.

EXPANSION OF SECULAR ROLE

Roman Catholics outnumbered Church of Ireland adherents by approximately 5: 1 according to Patrick O'Rourke's parish returns in 1834[27] (3,060 to 600). The first government census in which religious adherence received scrutiny was in 1861[28] and it revealed a similar ratio of 5 : 1 (1,578 to 305). By 1871[29] this Catholic majority had increased to 9 to 1 (1,571 to 177) probably caused by the departure of many English Protestant mill workers from the parish as is mentioned in the Church of Ireland papers of the time.[30] This growing majority coincided with a more liberal state approach towards the Roman Catholics as seen in the Catholic Emancipation Act 1828 and the 1869 Disestablishment of the Church of Ireland. This and the growing confidence of the church caused it to be drawn more into the secular affairs of the parish. The first evidence of this in the Catholic papers is to be found in March 1842 when the Poor Law Commission Office wrote to the archbishop of Dublin complaining that the parish priest of Celbridge, Fr. O'Rourke, had been offered by them the position of chaplain to the workhouse but that he had rejected the offer on financial grounds.[31] The workhouse system had been set up in 1838 to cater for the severely destitute. The Catholic church saw in the system many dangers including proselytism and Archbishop Cullen of Dublin was to call the workhouses 'an abomination, a sink of vice and misery'.[32] Despite this the Catholic hierarchy were prepared to allow priests to minister as workhouse chaplains provided that they (the hierarchy) retained the power to appoint and dismiss the chaplains. Fr. O'Rourke's rejection of the offer seems to have been solely because of his dissatisfaction with the annual salary on offer of £40. Archbishop Murray replied to the Commissioners as follows – 'if the Commissioners would think themselves able in this case to raise the salary to sixty pounds I would endeavour to induce Fr. O'Rourke to take a curate and accept the offer'.[33] These communications demonstrate the growing power of the Catholic Church. The workhouse had to have by law a Catholic chaplain and the state, in the form of the Board of the Poor Law Commission, would pay his salary. This new acceptance of the role of the Catholic clergy contrasts widely from their persecuted role in the previous century. This letter indicates that the archbishop was setting himself up as the authority which the Board must respect if they were to make progress in his diocese. Fr. O'Rourke however was not interested in the national implications of the argument – he simply wanted more money to cover his increased work-load. He did not get his £60 however and in fact according to Fr. John Donovan in 1880, the salary for workhouse chaplain was £50.[34] The archbishop however had made his point as to who would have control over the chaplains.

There is also a copy of an undated Poor Law Commissioners resolution where they were again pleading for the archbishop's intervention. The master (who managed the workhouse) stated that 'as the Roman Catholic service is given [in Celbridge workhouse] on Mondays, the greater number of inmates are necessarily unemployed on the morning of that day and that several of them are indisposed to doing their ordinary work during the remainder of the day.'[35] The Commissioners went on to ask for mass to be said on Sundays. One can only wonder whether it was devotion or clever manipulation of workhouse rules by the inmates which lay at the root of this problem? But again this amusing story points to the increased involvement of the Catholic Church in such institutions.

In 1870 a letter from a member of the Royal Irish Constabulary in Celbridge to Archbishop Cullen sought his intervention in seeking promotion 'some of my brother officers have even stronger claims as far as length of service is con-cerned but as there are only 3 Roman Catholic Head Inspectors for the whole island, the office is a most responsible one.'[36] The letter is interesting not only in so far as it tells us how much or how little progress had been made by Roman Catholics in securing the top positions in the public service but also because the writer believed that the patronage of the archbishop would be of help.

In January 1892 things had changed to the extent that we find Robert Kennedy, a Protestant member of the workhouse Board of Guardians writing to Archbishop Walsh – 'I most earnestly appeal to your Grace not to leave us out in the cold but to assist us in obtaining from your own diocese sisters of Mercy notably for the infirmary but also as Matron and another if possible to take charge of our schools. I can assure you that our Board will do everything you may require for increased accommodation for the sisters.'[37]

Robert Kennedy did in fact get his wish as the Sisters of Mercy were in-volved in the workhouse in many capacities until its closure by the Irish Free State in 1921.

The significant point in the episodes outlined in this section, is the grow-ing acceptance of such state bodies as the Board of Guardians and the Royal Irish Constabulary that they must cooperate with the Catholic church. At first this was a begrudging acceptance of the church's role and at no stage can any of these bodies be seen as reflecting the democratic wishes of the population of the parish – an issue which I will deal with in greater depth in the third chapter. But as can be seen by Robert Kennedy's letter, change was coming.

THE HUMAN STORY

Reading through the papers of the Catholic church in Celbridge there are occasions when brief human dramas unveil themselves before our eyes, giving the reader a feeling for the time and its people.

On 23 October 1835 a curate in the parish, a Rev. Costello, obviously distressed, wrote to the archbishop's secretary, Dr. Hamilton, complaining against 'the kind hearted pastor of Celbridge' (Fr. O'Rourke) whom he says 'charged him with what he had not done'.[38] 'On not a few occasions very plain hints were given whether they wish my departure or not I will not say. I may perhaps have mistaken them but me thinks I can say with truth I have not misconstrued them.' He went on to appeal to Dr. Hamilton to have him transferred without discussing the matter with the parish priest, Fr. O'Rourke. On 9 November 1835 he wrote again but this time with a great sense of urgency.[39] 'From the aspect of things here it occurs to me that it were better I should leave my present place as soon as possible, the sooner the better ... it were better in my mind to live a beggar than succumb to wrongful dark and ugly suspicions, when I speak of them covertly, but therefore not less pointedly, a burning face tells me his conviction that they are groundless and yet he treats me as if he were quite convinced of their truth. 'Tis strange!' This part of the sad little drama concluded thirteen days later when the parish priest informed Dr. Hamilton – 'Rev. Mr. Costello left on Saturday morning and took a boat from Hazelhatch [canal bridge about 1 mile from Celbridge] to Tullamore where he says he has relatives and with whom he told me he intends to stay until spring and then proceed to America to his father ... perhaps it is better that he should be with his own friends as he seemed to apprehend danger from almost everywhere – he even imagined the students from Maynooth had conspired against him.'[40] Although this was acted out in Celbridge 160 years ago, it is a story we could identify with quite easily today. People and their problems (self-made?) do not change. It also gives us an idea of the type of isolation which could be felt by a young priest as he tried to go about his ministry. Communications between Fr. Costello and his parish priest Fr. O'Rourke do not seem to have been good and it seems there was no place for the curate to seek help except from Dr. Hamilton, the archbishop's secretary. But help was not forthcoming here and the distressed curate felt that his only option was to leave the country. It can only be seen as a sad and lonely end to a young man's clerical vocation.

The divisive issue of private family property falling into the hands of a religious order is highlighted in 1867 when Charles Langdale, justice of the peace for East Yorkshire,[41] highly respected Catholic resident of Celbridge Abbey and son-in-law of Henry Grattan of Celbridge Abbey estate, wrote to Bishop Kilduff of Longford.[42] He informs the bishop that his sister-in-law Marian Grattan, had recently joined a religious order of nuns in the bishop's

diocese and that this order had subsequently laid claim to her portion of the
estate. As one of the trustees of Mr. Grattan's will he asked the bishop to encourage the nuns to withdraw this claim – 'thereby the many and deplorable
costs of litigation would be avoided.' He enclosed an extract of Henry Grattan's
will where he left his estates to his daughters – 'on the express condition that
none of them should enter or become a member of any convent of any such
religious society.[43]

Langdale concluded his appeal to the bishop 'the trustees are bound to act
– though you may believe that as a Catholic and as a relative, I shall thereby
be placed in a very painful position.' There followed a series of letters between
the two in which Bishop Kilduff endeavoured to have the matter settled pri-
vately. Langdale sought legal opinion on the idea of Marian taking her inher-
itance first and handing it all over to her religious community before her
profession. The letters concluded with Bishop Kilduff's expression of hope
that as he would be professing Marian on the following Friday – 'the community must only depend on the family to act honourably'.[44] He concludes –
'I am truly sorry not to have the pleasure of meeting you on Friday, (the day of
the profession). Did Henry Grattan's will succeed only in dividing the family?
Why all of this correspondence was kept in the archives of the archbishop of
Dublin we can only speculate but it is likely that it passed into the hands of
the archbishop, perhaps as a final arbitrator. This is in itself significant when
looking at the hierarchical structure among the Irish bishops. In this story we
have an example of the widespread fear that continues to this day that land
should pass out of the possession of the family. Henry Grattan wanted above
all, that his land would stay in the possession of his family after his death. This
clause in his will however was to divide his family and we can picture the
lonely daughter Marian, being professed as a nun, in the absence of her family
as mentioned in Bishop Kilduff's letter.

Both of the episodes described in this section I feel incorporate the more
human side of history into this study. Two sad human dramas which I hope,
have helped to make this story of religion in Celbridge, a story of real people.

EDUCATION

The Catholic church would seem to have been the church of the poor and
the uneducated. Many children were employed in the woollen mills in the
town. They received a payment of four shillings a week, when Edward
Wakefield inspected the factory in 1809.[45] Those who could afford to keep their
children away from such difficult employment also needed finance if they
wished to have their child educated. I have abstracted below some pertinent
data from the Commissioners of Irish Education Inquiry in 1826.[46] The number of pupils refer to an average from the three months prior to the government

assessment of educational facilities. I have not included Celbridge Charter school which had 126 female Protestant pupils, most from outside of the parish.

Parish of Celbridge

Number of Schools (all fee paying)	10
Average Daily Attendance of Catholics	255
Average Daily Attendance of Protestants	66
Number of Catholics attending schools catering for Catholic pupils only	120
Number of Catholics attending schools taught by a Protestant	27
Number of Catholics attending schools attended by Protestants also	135
Number of schools taught by Catholics	6
Number of schools taught by Protestants	4

It is interesting to note that more Catholics are attending schools of mixed denominations than those who attend schools teaching only Catholics. It is also worth noting that twenty seven Catholic pupils are paying a Protestant teacher to educate them. It is impossible to assess how many pupils are not receiving any education but if the 1821 census of the parish lists a total population of 1,949 there were more than 321 children of school going age in the parish.

If we are to accept the integrity of the parish reports, the Catholic church did place great emphasis on education. The *Catholic Directory* of 1821 reports that 400 children are given religious instruction each Sunday and also that 'an extensive school lately built by Right Hon. Lady Louisa Conolly for the instruction of poor children on the Lancastrian Plan, has a Catholic school master'.[47] The 1833 parish report informs us that there are four schools in the parish and the average number attending these schools is 250.[48] This would seem to be very small in particular if we accept the same priests census of his parish in 1834[49] as containing 3,826 Catholics. That the report states that these 250 were educated at the expense of their parents would indicate again that finance was perhaps the root of the problem. A letter of complaint against the parish priest in 1834 cites as his first neglect that there are 'no free Catholic schools'.[50] By 1839 the new parish priest (Fr. O'Rourke) had taken steps to ensure that the education of the parish's children is under stricter control of the church. He reported that there were two schools immediately under the patronage of the parish priest.[51] In these two parochial schools the parents partly paid and the parish priest paid where there was necessity. This is indeed an interesting development where the parish priest is seen to have diverted some of the very limited parish funds into the provision of education – even if it is only for a small number of children. The 1845 report[52] mentions, apart from schools kept at the expense of the mill-owners Shaw and Haughton and two schools kept by Colonel Conolly, a chapel school. The parish priest paid the teacher Mr. Kearnan £10 a year and the children attended without charge except for those who could afford to pay. The 1848[53] report goes into greater detail on the financing of this school – £10 a year was paid for Mr. Kearnan and because the school now seems to have moved to the chapel, there was also £10 a year rent paid on the building. This £20 was financed by £11 paid by the parish and £9 paid out of the legacy of Mrs. King. A copy of Mrs. King's will shows that she bequested 'to the Rev. P. Brennan (P.P. 1802–1821) the sum of £300 ... to apply it for the purpose it was intended ... that is the establishment of a school for poor children in the town'.[54]

Despite the self-congratulatory nature of these reports the education of Catholics was less than adequate during the first four decades of the century. It seems clear that very many children received little or no education. Evidence of this appears in Fr. O'Rourke's parish report of 1845 – 'There is also evening instruction given in both chapels from the months of April until October in catechism [religious instruction], spelling and reading which is very useful and important to the poorer kind of children who have to work and cannot attend the day school'.[55] The extent or this part-time education is revealed when he explained that an average of about 100 attend the chapel day school whereas this evening school has an average attendance of up to 300. All of this evidence points to the poverty of the families and a widespread educational neglect. What is surprising is that the state was willing to fund schools (even under Catholic managers) since the setting up of the National School system in 1831 and yet no parish priest in Celbridge applied to the Board of Education for the establishment of such a school.

The setting up of the National School System in 1831 was in the end to prove a great asset for the provision of education to poor Catholics. Corish says 'ironically perhaps the new state system restored to the Catholic church a great deal of the control over the primary school system which it had been in danger of losing'.[56] In most cases it was the Catholic priest who applied for the school and became its manager. In Celbridge however this was not the case. The first school to be set up in the village under the new national system was the Abbey National School. In 1848 Henry Grattan, son of the famous Henry Grattan the parliamentarian, applied for and received aid towards the building of this school.[57] Grattan, a prominent landlord who had married a Catholic, thus became the patron of the Abbey Boys School and the Abbey Girls School. In 1855 Grattan appointed his son-in-law, Charles Langdale, as manager. The abbey evening school was set up to cater for pupils employed in the mills during the day.[58] The Abbey Infant School was also established in 1857 and the Inspector's report at the time said 'an infant school is most beneficial in any town but especially in Celbridge – the majority of adults are employed daytime in the mills and cannot execute control over them'.[59] This comment on Celbridge as it was at the time, would perhaps shatter any illusions we may hold of a more disciplined society in Victorian days. By the middle of the 1860s all three schools had come under the management of the parish priest though they remained under the patronage of Charles Langdale, Grattan's successor. In fact when Rev. Myles McManus resigned as parish priest and school manager in 1873, Mr. Langdale wrote to the Board of Education and insisted that a manager be not appointed without his permission.[60] When this was accepted by the Board he then proceeded to appoint the next parish priest, Fr. John Donovan, as manager.

It is difficult to understand the implications behind Charles Langdale's insistence that he and the Grattan family would retain control over the appointment of a school manager. Perhaps he wished to establish clearly their rights as school-founders and owners of the property on which the school was built.

Despite having a priest as manager the national schools were strictly non-denominational. Religious instruction had to be clearly time tabled in these schools run under the Board of Education and was kept quite separate from the teaching of all other subjects. In 1877 the manager of the Abbey Boys School wrote to the Board seeking permission to deviate temporarily from the school timetable so that he might take the children to the chapel to prepare for their confirmation.[61] Permission was granted provided that one teacher remained in school lest any child should not wish to go to the chapel. In 1880 the Abbey Girls School closed and the girls were transferred to the new convent school.[62] Unfortunately there are no records in the Holy Faith Sisters archives for the early years of this school. In the final decades of the century the village had organised, regulated and funded schools courtesy of the Board of Education but with the parish priest as manager. The very demographics of the village were such that though these schools were in name non-denominational, they were almost exclusively Catholic. As William Thackeray said when he visited Ireland in 1879 – 'Look at the national school throughout the country. It is commonly by the chapel side – it is a Catholic school directed and fostered by the priest; and as no people are more eager for learning, more apt to receive it or more grateful for kindness than the Irish, he gets all the gratitude of the scholars who flock to the school'.[63]

Education could not have been a priority for poor families who were trying to survive. The surviving papers of the Catholic church in Celbridge refer a lot to education but in fact the church's performance in this areas was quite weak. It was left to the benevolent Protestant landlords to take the initiative – people such as the Conollys and the Grattans. The situation was changing slowly for the better however and an analysis of the census returns for Celbridge workhouse in 1901 confirms this.[64] At the time of the census there

were 166 paupers in the workhouse and of these only thirty-three were
deemed to be illiterate. When we remember that these poor people were the
most disadvantaged group in society at the time, the fact that 133 of them
could read or read and write, was an indication of progress.

FINANCE

Unfortunately there are no financial records or accounts for the Catholic
parish of Celbridge in the nineteenth century. The only exception to this is
the ledger book kept by Fr. Daniel Byrne in which he recorded the receipts
and expenditure on parochial buildings from 1855 to 1868.[65] It is possible to
piece together information taken from the general collection of parish letters
etc. to give an indication as to the general financial situation in the parish.

It is obvious from the parish reports of the 1820s and 1830s that finance
was in short supply. The necessity of sharing a ciborium and some of the vest-
ments between both chapels would be but one indication of this. However,
the fact that both chapel houses were free of any rent must certainly have
been a relief on finances. The chapel house itself was described by Fr. Byrne
in 1856 as 'this wretched chapel which everyone pronounces a disgrace to the
diocese'.[66] This must again point towards the poverty experienced by the
church in the first half of the century. There is also a letter from curate Patrick
Woods to the archbishop in 1844 in which he says 'I have repeatedly called
Fr. O'Rourke's attention to the state of the Straffan chapel and I shall not
trouble your Grace with the replies – suffice to say that for want of a few
spouts the foundation walls and the doors are eaten away'.[67] In his letter however he goes on to banish any idea that the poor state of the church is the result
of shortage of finance – 'the district cannot be so poor when their offerings
on Christmas day average £12 – but it is not the fault of the people'. It is
interesting to see the memorandum attached by Fr. Lynch to his letter of
complaint against Fr. O'Rouke, P.P. in 1854.[68] I have abbreviated Fr. Lynch's
memorandum to illustrate his estimates of parish finances.

Collected at Straffan church	(over 21 months)	£37–16–0
Collected at Celbridge church	(over 16 months)	£112–0–0
Salary from Workhouse	(21 months)	£70–0–0
	Total	£219–16–0
Fr. Lynch claimed one third of this		£73–5–4

Fr. O'Rourke had in fact only paid his curate a total of £33 and so not for the
first time Fr. O'Rourke was in conflict with his curate. It would seem that a
shortage of money and indeed disputes about money were a regular feature

of clerical life in Celbridge, if we are to accept what we read in the church's papers. Fr. Lynch believed in this instance that the money collected from both churches would have provided a reasonable income for the parish priest and himself if only Fr. O'Rourke was willing to divide it fairly. The parish at this time was not paying any pension to the previous parish priest, Fr. Murphy, whose early retirement I discussed above. He had in fact died shortly after his retirement in 1841.

Perhaps the greatest insight we can get into the finances of the parish is to be found in a fascinating book now in the church in Celbridge. It was commenced on the 21 October 1855 by the then parish priest, Rev. Daniel Byrne, and gives the most minute detail, the receipts and expenditure on parochial buildings from 1855 to 1868.[69]

The story opens with the collection and expenditure of £101 9s. 0d. on repairs to the old church carried out in the closing months of 1855. No sooner was this work completed than Fr. Byrne embarked on the building of a new school at Straffan – a solid two-storey structure still in use – which cost the unbelievable figure of £254 and which was completed and paid for by the end of 1857. This zealous pastor did not neglect the mother church in Celbridge and we read that on 15 May 1858 he had opened a subscription list for a 'new church of Saint Patrick, Celbridge'.

More than sixty closely written pages follow, meticulously registering literally every shilling subscribed for the new church. On the opposite pages appears a complete record of expenditure. Under the date 21 January 1862 the credit and debit balance of the account agree on the figure of £4,869 17s. 9d. and the old man enters a triumphant 'Laus Deo Semper' (Praise God forever). The original estimate for the building was £3,450 12s. 10d. and the actual cost including altars, statues, confessionals and stained glass windows, together with seating amounted to the incredible figure shown above – £4,869 17s. 4d. A further expenditure of £220 provided the magnificent pulpit and baptism font, both in cut stone, and some additional seating. Collection for the church began in 1856 and the entire work was paid within six years.

The new church was described in the *Irish Builder* at the time (1859) as follows – 'It is the early pointed style of the thirteenth century comprising nave, chancel and side aisles with votive chapels, one dedicated to the Virgin Mary and the other to the Holy Sacrament'.[70] The architect was the highly respected J.J. McCarthy who afterwards designed the chapel of St. Patrick's College, Maynooth.[71]

Fr. Byrne however was still not satisfied. In July 1863 he commenced collecting for the new parochial house and by the time of his retirement in October 1864 he had gathered £446 11s. 6d. He had borrowed £500 and the actual work on the house when it was completed in December of 1866 came to a total cost of £1,236. Compared to the cost of the church (£4,869) this may seem a lot but the house itself is very big, positioned directly opposite the

Church of Ireland and the gates of Castletown House. The construction by the Catholic parishioners of this impressive house for their priest was obviously a matter in which they took great pride.

An analysis of Fr. Byrne's receipts columns reveals some of his secrets. First, it was advisable to succeed a generous P.P. Fr. Byrne's predecessor, Fr. Patrick O'Rourke left 'shares in the new 3 per cent stock, which realised £1,561 7s. od. This may explain why Fr. O'Rourke was so often in dispute with his curates regarding money. Secondly one must not be a discriminator of persons when seeking funds. Fr. Byrne obtained money from the Kirkpatrick's – a Presbyterian family. He also records two other entries – 31 March 1857 – John Coughlin (his first prize at school) one shilling and under 6 May 1858 – the police ten shillings. Nobody escaped his attentions, the architect paid £35 and his curate paid for a stained glass window. Fr. Byrne was himself generous and contributed about £80 and a stained glass window.

Thirdly he saw the value of advertising and several entries refer to advertisements he placed in the *Freeman's Journal*. He ran a special train from Dublin for the official opening of the church and finally he seems to have charged ten shillings for admission to the opening. He also employed a raffle as a method of fund-raising and he realised £46 18s. od. by this method in November 1857. The grand prize for this raffle was a copy of *The Lives of the Saints*.[72]

Two entries written by Fr. Byrne himself in the ledger book capture the enthusiasm, happiness and dedication of this man on 19 December 1858. 'Mass was said today (for the first time) in the new church. Collection £22 – 19 June 1859. This day the church was blessed by the Right Rev. Moriarty, bishop of Kerry (in the absence of His Grace the archbishop of Dublin from illness). The Right Rev. Dr. McNally, bishop of Clogher and the Right Rev. Dr. Whelan, bishop of Bombay, being present with a large number of priests and an immense concourse of the laity, Laus Deo Semper, D.V.'

Given the poverty of the parish as already described Fr. Daniel Byrne's magnificent accomplishments in such a short time require explanation. Certainly he was dynamic but he also seems to have had the support of his entire parish. The benevolent landlord Charles Langdale (Grattan's Catholic son-in-law) for example provided all the limestone for the church free of charge. He was also lucky to undertake his building programme when the population of the parish was at its height because of the mills which continued to thrive until the early 1870s. It must have been a source of great pride for these (mostly) poor Catholics to have at last a large and beautiful church erected at the centre point of the town's main street. This and the significant erection of the magnificent priests house overlooking the Protestant church, had a significance which nobody could overlook. Times were certainly changing!

But those days of great achievement were to pass – perhaps because of the decline of the mills but also surely because of the departure of the dynamic Fr. Byrne. On January 3rd 1890 Fr. Donovan P.P. wrote to the archbishop –

'I wrote to your Grace for an exemption for this parish for the collection about to be made for the poor of Ireland … Both factories are now closed, 800 to 900 hands thrown idle with their families, more than half our population. Their receipts per week used to be £400. All of this was spent in this locality – a great sum in a small place. Our Catholic population is of the very poorest, scarcely a dozen are comfortable … all were nearly dependent on the factories. The people still give as they can yet our collection is not much more than half of what it used to be'.[73] Later in his letter we learn that the previous complacency towards the position of the workhouse chaplain has gone – 'The Union is £50 a year and only for it two priests could not live here'.

The material is not available to analyse the Catholic church's finances in great detail but it has been possible to provide a general overall picture. The first fifty years of the nineteenth century would seem to have been years of slow improvement in parish finances. Those years were difficult especially for the priests who worked in the parish. But the 1850s and 1860s were as we have seen, years of great accomplishment for the parish. What evidence we have would seem to indicate that the final three decades of the nineteenth century were years of poverty and hardship for the Catholic church and Celbridge in general.

CONCLUSION

Before drawing any conclusions to this chapter I think it is important to comment on three of the parish priests who helped shape the development of the Catholic church in Celbridge.

Father Patrick O'Rourke was parish priest of Celbridge from 1833 to 1855. He was in many ways a controversial figure as we have seen, coming into conflict with his curates on more than one occasion. Money was often the cause of these conflicts and there is even an account in the *Dublin Evening Post* on 7 May 1842 of a court case where his niece is accused of stealing £1,000 from him while acting as his housekeeper.[74] Even after his death (1855) there are a number of letters surviving and from these it would seem that his brothers and sisters are in financial hardship and expect assistance from the church.[75] Nevertheless Fr. Daniel Byrne his successor was to benefit from Fr. O'Rourke's financial schemes when he collected over £1,500 that O'Rourke had left in shares and which provided a great impetus to the church building fund.

Father Daniel Byrne (P.P. 1855–1865) would seem to have been a most dynamic and astute individual. When I asked an older member of Celbridge's present day community why she thought that the poor people of the parish built such a magnificent parochial house for their parish priest, she replied that priests in those days were held in very high esteem and nothing would have been considered too good for a man like Daniel Byrne.

Father Henry Murphy was parish priest from 1889–1892 and though I could find little information about him, I was very impressed by the loving and meticulous way he copied and restored the oldest parish registers. He has, like his fellow parish priests, left his mark.

The picture of the Catholic parish of Celbridge I hope is now more clear. It is a picture of a church of poor people struggling to survive and to improve their lot.

They were Catholics living in a society largely controlled by Protestants but their church was gradually beginning to assert itself. They were led by priests upon whom they depended a great deal and whom they held in high regard. It is a picture of real people – who though struggling to survive themselves, still continued to work for the improvement of their church.

The Church of Ireland

It is perhaps a reflection on the organised character and nature of the Church of Ireland, that such thorough records on its past are available. I hope in this chapter to outline the main features of this well organised church and track its development through the nineteenth century. However, though it is well served by formal records such as Select Vestry minutes from 1813 to 1900, Accounts books from 1846 to 1882 and preacher books from 1871 to 1905, it is lacking in papers of a non-formal or personal nature. This chapter surveys the structure of the Church of Ireland in Celbridge, it's finances, involvement in education and in the society that was nineteenth century Celbridge. It also examines in some detail the minute book of Celbridge Young Men's Christian Association which survives for the period March 1862 until May 1863. I hope that by piecing together the information from these various aspects of the Church of Ireland, I will help to create a fuller picture of this numerically small but important religious community.

ORGANISATION

In the parish of Celbridge the names commonly used to denote a person's religious adherence would be Catholic meaning Roman Catholic and Protestant meaning Church of Ireland. The term Protestant of course could apply to many other church bodies such as Methodist or Presbyterian. However as the number of adherents in Celbridge to any Protestant church other than the Church of Ireland was always very small I shall use the commonly used term Protestant to signify the church now officially called the Church of Ireland. The 1871 census recorded thirty-six Protestants in Celbridge[1] who were not members of the Church of Ireland. The corresponding figure in 1901 was nineteen.[2]

The term 'Church of Ireland' did not become the sole official title for the Anglican Communion until after the Disestablisment Act of 1869.[3] During the period 1800–1869 the correct title for the church was 'The United Church of England and Ireland' though in most documentation is referred to as the 'Established Church'. The common title for the parish in use for most of the century, was 'the parish of Kildrought' even though it was like the Catholic church, a union of parishes – having incorporated Straffan prior to 1800. Prior to 1798, the community worshipped in the church of St. Mochua in Church Lane but according to some sources this was burnt during the rebel-

33

lion and service was held at Castletown House for about fourteen years.[4] The predecessor of the present church was build around 1812 and the first vestry minutes available are dated 9 November 1813.[5] The select vestry is a governing body of each parish who looked after the buildings, finance, education and other day to day concerns of the parish. It was composed of, as we shall see later, elected parishioners usually respected men of property. At times in the early years of the century it had an almost civil role as regards looking after the poor of the parish until the workhouse system was established in 1838. The building of the church had been completed thanks to 'several sums of £500 and one thousand pounds lent free of interest by the board of first fruits to the parishioners of Kildrought and Straffan'.[6] The board of first fruits were a part of the overall governing body of the Established Church and were empowered to lend money to individual parishes for construction of new churches such as this. To repay this money the select vestry proposed the 'sale and appropriation of the said seats in the said church'.[7]

Each of the prominent landowners acquired the best pews for instance the earl of Leitrim, who lived at Kiladoon just outside the village, paid £64 over sixteen years for his. Six of these pews even had their own fireplaces. By 1881 this building was in a poor state of repair and the vestry minutes of 2 May 1882 record the receipt of an offer from the mill-owner Mr. Shaw of £1,000 for the restoration of the building.[8] A tender of £2,069 was accepted for the proposed alterations and £20 was to be spent on the school so that worship could be held there during the alterations to the church.[9] The select vestry meeting of 28 July 1884 resolved that Kildrought Church be consecrated in the name of Christ Church, Celbridge and that consecration would take place in September.[10] The *Irish Builder* described the renovated church as 'Gothic style – consisting of a nave 60 ft by 25 ft with an aisle on the north side and a chancel 28ft by 21ft'.[11]

As can be seen from Canon J.B. Leslie's biographical succession list of the clergy[12] the parish during the century was served by a total of four vicars assisted each by one curate until 1874.

Vicars of the Parish of Kildrought (Celbridge)

1786 to 1801	Beather King
1801 to 1829	Patrick Sandys
1829 to 1881	Robert Pakenham
1881 to 1911	Charles Graham

There are few documents surviving that provide any personal insight into the first two incumbents (the term often used officially to denote vicar). Robert Pakenham, a relative of the influential Conolly family, was a highly important character in the life of the parish, acting as vicar for all of fifty-two years. The lack of any personal papers such as letters means that it is difficult to get to know more about his character or that of his successor Charles Graham. However at the chapter's conclusion I intend to draw together any information available on these two men.

A study of the Preacher's Books which are in existence from 1861 show that service was held twice each Sunday and once on holy days. The Church of Ireland population of the parish of Celbridge was estimated by Catholic parish priest Fr. O'Rourke as being 610 in 1834.[13] According to the Church of Ireland's own visitation records[14] the size of the congregation was in decline – from 1881 when it numbered 294 to a figure of 200 in the year 1900.

The following material summarised from the baptism and marriage registers of the Church of Ireland should illustrate the church's population trends in the nineteenth century.

Years	Registered Baptisms	Registered Marriages
1801–1810	106	14
1811–1820	188	24
1821–1830	178	31
1831–1840	151	26
1841–1850	98	29
1851–1860	97	26
1861–1870	80	21
1871–1880	67	13
1881–1890	33	16
1891–1900	29	20

As can be seen from this the peak period for baptisms in the parish were the years 1811 to 1820. From that period on there is a steady decline which becomes a severe decline in the 1880s. The figures for marriages are much more consistent throughout the century and are actually on the increase at the century's end. As was the case in the Catholic church the declining baptism figures after the 1870s can best be accounted for by declines in the mills. Similarly the high baptism figures in the early decades may be related to the number of English Protestants who were brought over to work in and instruct in these woollen mills. Many of these English Protestants were housed in a long row of houses directly opposite the mills and their custom of throwing tea-leaves out onto the lane-way at the rear of the cottages, caused this lane to be known as Tea Lane to this day. Considering the relatively small numbers it is obvious that the parishioners were well served with a vicar and a curate prior to 1880 and a vicar only from that year on.

Men who served as Curates in Parish of Kildrought (Celbridge)

1798–1803	Newcomen Whitelaw
1803–1820	Anthony Hastings
1820–1836	Samuel Greer
1836–1861	John Crawford
1861–1864	Marcus John Bickerstaff
1870–1874	Aiken Irvine

But small though the congregation may have been there can be no doubt of their pride in their parish and their determination not to have their boundaries encroached on. The vestry minutes of 25 October 1871 record the outrage at the proposed union with the nearby parish of Newcastle – 'we instruct our representatives at the Synod of Glendalough to express our deep astonishment that such a proposition should have been made ... and that though Celbridge is by far the larger and more influential parish it was left in ignorance of such a proposal. As a parish having a large residential church population who are willing to contribute liberally to the support of the Church of Ireland, we respectfully desire to enter a most decided protest against any such union'.[15] It is most interesting to note the use of the words 'who are willing to contribute liberally to the support of the Church' as it would seem to imply a threat or at least it holds out the possibility of more money being available to the church if the wishes of the select vestry are complied with.

Surprisingly there is only one recorded communication between the archbishop of Dublin and the Celbridge select vestry and this was on the minor matter of requesting that insurance on the church building be taken out against fire.[16] This request from the archbishop was read to the select vestry at its annual meeting in April of 1860 but in fact insurance was not taken out until 1871 when the church was insured to a value of £2,000 which included a harmonium insured at £50.[17] Perhaps this absence of correspondence from (or mention of) the archbishop is a weakness in the surviving parish records but it is more likely to indicate a church much more autonomous than it's Catholic counterpart. Power seemed to have rested to a great degree in the hands of the parishioners and their elected select vestry. The select vestry, which consisted of the most influential and wealthy men in the parish, would seem to have wielded almost total control over church affairs throughout the century. If we look at the people who formed the select vestry at any one year and then search out their names and places of abode in the relevant directory for that year we can see the status of the people involved.

Select Vestry 1876[18] –

Thomas Conolly, M.P., Castletown House
Edward Cane, J.P., St. Wolstan's Abbey

Alexander Kirkpatrick, J.P., Donacomper House
Colonel Clements, the earl of Leitrim, Killadoon House
John Maunsell Esq, J.P., Oakley Park
Robert Whitelaw Esq, Ardrass Lodge, Celbridge
Joseph Shaw, Millowner, Barberstown Castle

Here in the first seven names mentioned we have, according to the *Salters Directory*,[19] the owners of all the major landed estates in the parish bar one (Celbridge Abbey which was owned by a Roman Catholic, General Richard Dease). Throughout the century the same family names occur on the lists of select vestry but the name Conolly always seems to have taken precedent. It must be remembered that the church was actually built on land given free by the Conolly family at the beginning of the century and located symbolically within the entrance gates to their demesne. When the select vestry met in July 1870 to tackle the financial implications of disestablishment (the 1869 act of parliament which removed the church from its position as the state or established church) it was Tom Conolly (1823–1876) who pledged £1,000 towards the future financing of the church.[20] It is not surprising then that his name was first on the list of select vestrymen elected each year or that a special meeting was called on 20 November 1876 to offer sympathy to Mrs. Conolly 'in the great affliction in consequences of the death of her late husband'.[21] Again the esteem in which the family are held is reflected in the special meeting which was held on 1 September 1891[22] for the purpose of congratulating young Thomas Conolly on the occasion of his attaining his majority. On 30 May 1895[23] we find the same Thomas Conolly asking and receiving from the select vestry permission to have a portion of ground behind the church consecrated as a private burial ground for his family.

Throughout the century the same family names keep cropping up as members of the select vestry – Maunsell, Johnston, Cane, Shaw, Clements, Kirkpatrick. Again this should not seem surprising when we remember that the Church of Ireland was a small community as can be seen from the figures below.

1834	Estimate of Fr. O'Rourke[24] (it would seem to err on high side)	600
1861	Census[25]	305
1871	Census[26]	177
1881	Parish Records[27]	294
1891	Parish Records[28]	200
1900	Parish Records[29]	200

The parish records would have included people living outside the parish who were considered members of the regular congregation. Within this small community was the even smaller group from which the select vestry came – the select group of men of wealth and property. As mentioned already this represented almost all of the major landed estates in the area.

Most of the matters dealt with by the select vestry concerned the routine management of the church. The select vestry met usually in April of each year but if necessary met on more than one occasion to deal with any pressing matter. The only time this occurred prior to disestablishment was in 1828, 1830 and 1831 when the vestry met in special session to meet with delegations from adjoining parishes to negotiate tithe composition. The minutes of the annual meetings were brief and though the rector attended it would seem that he was there to report on affairs of the parish and to note the decisions of the select vestry – an observer more than an active participant. For the first seventy years the minutes record an array of trivial affairs dealt with by the annual vestry – the purchase and payment of pews, the allocation of funds for the purchase of coffins for the poor.

The affairs dealt with by the vestry were usually financial in nature and each year's minutes up to disestablishment, contain an agreed estimate of expenditure for the coming year and the agreed applotment of tithes which would have to be raised to cover this expenditure. A typical example is shown below.

1825 Schedule of Sums to be Raised

Clerk's Salary	£20
Bell Ringer's Salary	£4
Sectoness's Salary	£10
Instalment of Board of First Fruits	£10
Bread and Wine	£4
Contingencies	£20
Poundage to Collectors of Tithes	£3 8s od
Total	£71 8s 0s

However, the church was to undergo a major upheaval with the disestablishment of the church. Prior to the passing of the act, the church was in fact part of the apparatus of government. The church up until the 1830s had been funded by the collection of tithes from the people of all creeds in the parish. After the 1838 Tithe Act these tithes were replaced by land rents collected by the state from the landowners and paid to the church. According to Akenson the Established Church paid a price for its state support – 'Before 1869 the Church of Ireland was an open organisation system – Parliament could meddle at will with its structures, finances and theology'.[30] After disestablishment the church was to stand on its own financial and administrative feet. The select vestry in Celbridge seems to have seen this change as a challenge and in their first meeting under the new circumstances they passed the following resolution – 'Having regard to the duties and responsibilities entailed upon the Protestants of Ireland by the altered circumstances of our church at large and also with a view to meeting the necessities of our immediate case we resolve ... '[31] They go on to draw up financial plans to cope with their new situation. The disestablishment measures had made provision for the mainte- nance of all the present incumbents of the church but after their passing each parish had to make provision for their replacement – this was done by the Sustentation Fund – 'Being the amount required to be paid in each successive year to secure for Celbridge, in the event of the parish becoming vacant, stipends for a rector of £250 per annum and for a curate of £100 per annum'.[32] The collection for this Sustentation Fund was divided into two sections – Section 1 – annual lump sum payments by the wealthy and Section II – card collections by the poorer families and Protestant servants of the big houses. It is interesting to look at the figures for the early years of this fund.[33]

Year	Section I	Section II	Total
1872	£184	£11	£195
1873	£204	£18	£222
1874	£175	£20	£195
1875	£174	£6	£180

Again we can see that the individual contributions of the wealthy (Section 1) far out-stripped the contributions of the more numerous poorer parishioners (Section II). Satisfactory though this response was the vestry were ever mind- ful of savings and the minutes of 12 January 1880 record – 'when disestablish- ment took place in 1870 the population included the hands of two large flax-mills – mainly being Protestant. These mills having been closed without any prospect of being re-opened and the vestry are of the unanimous opinion that the necessity for having a curate no longer exists – no curate having been in the parish since about 1874'.[34] They proceeded to seek and were granted a reduction in their payment to the sustentation fund.

The fears of what disestablisment might do to the church seems to have reinvigorated interest in and attendance at select vestry meetings. The select vestry was usually attended by about twelve people including the vicar and the two church wardens would also attend. Although the minutes would detail the names of the elected vestry, these names did not vary much from year to year and it would seem unlikely that there was much of an electoral contest to secure a seat. They were elected by the general body of parishioners called the general vestry. However after the disestablishment of the church a new se- lect vestry minute book was opened (1870 to 1893) and it recorded in great detail the minutes of this first meeting of the now independent church. It opened with a list of all the vestrymen (the general vestry) – their numbers now swollen to about 100. It stated their qualification and place of residence. Some of those listed were in fact not permanent residents of the parish but were regular attendants at the church. Such was the enthusiasm engendered by Disestablishment that there was even a recorded election for one of the two positions of church wardens – the second warden was nominated by the rector.

In fact disestablishment seems to have given the church members the impetus to improve their parish e.g. 1881 provision of parish school,[35] 1884 major renovation of church building,[36] 1890 purchase of Celbridge lodge as a Glebe house.[37] All of these decisions were taken by the lay people of the select vestry and in fact the minutes fail to mention the vicar except when he is directed to do something. Disestablishment would seem to have increased even further the power of the elected select vestry.

Sadly the enthusiastic attendances did not continue and it is mentioned in the vestry minutes of 1 June 1885 that the custom is now to re-elect the vestry of the previous year if they are willing to accept the position. Towards the end of the 1880s and in the 1890s many men who had served on the select vestry for many years receive their last mention in the vestry minutes:

12/4/1887	The select vestry expresses its regret at the death of George Maunsell.[38]
27/6/1887	The select vestry expresses its regret at the death of Joseph Shaw.[39]
10/3/1891	The select vestry expresses its regrets at the deaths of Alex Kirkpatrick and Richard Cane.[40]

The passing of these stalwart vestrymen combined with the declining Protestant population (already illustrated earlier) must have placed greater strains on those who continued to manage the affairs of the parish.

The Church of Ireland was a more compact organisation, than its Catholic counterpart. It was well managed by the select vestry which consisted mainly of the wealthy and powerful people of the parish. The church was served by four men who ministered to the parishioners at different periods during the century and these men were supported by curates until 1874 when the declining congregations removed the necessity for this. The vicars do not seem to have at any state had the administrative responsibilities which the parish priests carried in the Catholic church. It was in many ways a smaller, more democratic and perhaps better organised church.

THE YOUNG MEN'S CHRISTIAN ASSOCIATION

A branch of the Young Men's Christian Association was set up in Celbridge in 1862 with Thomas Conolly as patron. The object of the Association was 'to unite its members in the bonds of Christian sympathy and to promote the spiritual, intellectual and social improvement of the young men of Celbridge'.[41] Admission to the association was to be open to all young men who could provide a satisfactory certificate of character from their employer. The first meeting was hosted by Giles Shaw, the mill-owner, in Celbridge Lodge and forty-one members paid their two and six pence annual membership.

The reason why such a group was established at this time is open to speculation. The 1860s, as has been shown earlier, was a time when the population of the town was high (1,883 in 1861 census) and the Church of Ireland baptism and marriage figures as already illustrated were also high. The town would seem to have been prospering thanks to the mills and the Roman Catholic church as shown in the first chapter had just built a new church (1859) and was about to begin collecting for a new and elaborate parochial house for its parish priest (collection initiated July 1863). Perhaps this new found confidence among Catholics was one reason for the initiation of this Association. Certainly the host of the meeting Giles Shaw, the mill owner, had been seen by Catholic curate Fr. Lynch in his letter dated 2nd May 1854 as a proselytiser.[42] So we may assume that Shaw was an enthusiastic supporter of his church and saw in the Y.M.C.A. as a means of strengthening the religious beliefs of the young Protestants of the town. It also became a place of social contact for young Protestant men and as we shall see from the list of lectures given at their meetings, it was to have an educational content as well. Giles Shaw even provided rooms in his mills where the Association could meet.

The minutes of these meetings are all quite brief and seem to be written in the rather pompous tones which would have been common among the better educated classes at the time. For instance they refer to each other as 'Mr.', a practice we would not now expect of young men. The meetings at first were held on a weekly basis and began with a reading of scripture. Church support for the Association can be seen by the presence of the vicar Rev. Packenham at the first public meeting held on 24 March 1862.

The lecture topics for these meetings reveals a lot about the concerns and interests of these young men and the aims of the organisation. These topics, which were in most cases given by members of the Association, show their interest in science and religion. A library room was also opened for the group and subscriptions were taken out and orders were placed for such journals as *The Mechanic's magazine* and *The Illustrated London News*.

All would seem to have been gong well with the Association until the meeting of 16 April 1862. A Mr. Wingfield read an essay that night on education.[43] A member Thomas Arbuthnot declared that he could not agree with the contents of Mr. Wingfield's essay and he promised that he would prepare his own essay on the topic. Was it a coincidence that on the same night a vote was held on the subject of bringing strangers to meetings and that the vote was against such? Who these strangers were we are not informed but the very fact that a

Date	Topic
02/04/1862	Intellectual Excellence
09/04/1862	Missionary Work to the Jews
16/04/1862	Education
07/05/1862	The Advantages of Steam Power to Great Britain
16/05/1862	Our Earth and its satellites
28/05/1862	Greatness of Character
04/06/1862	Time
18/06/1862	The Jews
02/07/1862	Self-knowledge
23/07/1862	The Microscope
13/08/1862	The Evils of Civil War
24/08/1862	The Value of Unity
17/09/1862	Intemperance
05/11/1862	True Womanhood

vote had to be taken shows an element of division in this fledgling organisation. Presumably the strangers referred to were not Catholics but rather Protestants who had not paid their annual membership fee. Perhaps there was an element of class conflict as we read later that members who could not pay the full membership at once would be allowed to pay in instalments. Three months later Thomas Arbuthnot arrived at a meeting with his essay on education prepared but after a vote of the meeting he was denied permission to read it.[44] The row that ensued caused Arbuthnot to resign as secretary three weeks later.[45] Days after this when the essay to be read was ironically 'The value of unity', a letter from Thomas Shaw was received resigning from the Association.[46] This caused consternation in the group and a delegation was dispatched to ask him to change his mind. On 3 September the delegation reported that they had met young Shaw 'under the counsel of his father, Giles Shaw, the mill-owner'.[47] Eventually Shaw agreed to come back on the condition that Thomas Arbuthnot be re-elected and this was done on 17 September 1862. From that night on however the intervals between meetings grew greater, their reading room closed and on 7 April 1863 a letter from Shaw was received in which he declared that circumstances had occurred which prevented him attending any further meetings except those open to the public.[48] The next meeting on 6 May was the final meeting recorded.

It is possible that, as young Shaw was now withdrawing his support from the Association, it was unlikely that his father would have been willing to continue to provide the use of rooms for the Association. Unfortunately the minutes are written in such a polite manner as not to give the details of any disputes which were taking place. We are left to guess as to the answer to the intriguing question – 'What was the real reason for the Association's break-up?' Was there a clash between the wealthier and poorer members? Who were these strangers that Shaw so wished to have access to the meetings?

The setting up of the Association was significant in that it illustrates the sufficient availability of potential members. The tone of the minutes also revealed a certain confidence among the Protestant community in their religion and also to some degree it demonstrated a sense of self-assurance by the upper classes. The Association's early demise must have been a severe disappointment to the same church and social class.

FINANCE

There is a large amount of material available for an analysis of the finances of the Church of Ireland in nineteenth century Celbridge. Because of the changing circumstances in which the church operated – with and without tithes, as an established state church, as an independent church after 1869 – its financial affairs are highly intricate. These changing circumstances make it difficult to compare the financial data of different periods within the nineteenth century. I shall divide my analysis into two areas – pre and post disestablishment, the sources used here are the select vestry minutes 1813 to 1893, the Preacher's books 1861 to 1905, Celbridge Poor Accounts 1846 to 1860 and Celbridge Holy Communion book for the same years 1846 to 1860. The first of the select vestry minute books (1813 to 1870) opens with the assembly of the first select vestry elected in the parish since the erection of the new church in 1812.[49] The business of this first meeting dated 9 November 1813 was to make provision for the payment of the building costs of the church. The Board of First Fruits, as mentioned earlier, had lent Kildrought parish a sum of £1,000 for this purpose and it was agreed to repay this loan in instalments. To raise this money the select vestry intended to auction the pews in the church and it was obviously a matter of great prestige to secure one of the better pews. The vestry minutes then listed the purchasers of the different pews in their place of dwelling. It is worth identifying some of these important parishioners because it gives an indication of the potential of wealth available to the Church of Ireland at that time.

These families, as set out below, were almost all of the landed gentry in the parish and its surrounds. These same family names are to be found as part of the select vestry right to the century's end. Each family was to pay for their pew over a period of sixteen years. The earl of Leitrim for example who acquired pew number one with its own fireplace (one of six such pews) was to pay £64 in total for his pew. The total annual sum to be collected annually for the pews was £60 7s. 2d.[50] However, some people did not continue their annual repayments and others who left the parish had their seats re-claimed by

Name	*Address*
Col. Clements, earl of Leitrim	Kiladoon House
William Kirkpatrick	Rockfield House
Arthur Henry	Lodge Park
John Cooper	Roselawn House
Conolly Family (who purchased 2 pews)	Castletown House
The Duke of Leinster	Carton House, Maynooth
(seat to be used by visitors)	
William Shaw (mill owner)	Temple Mills
Jeremiah Haughton	Celbridge Factory Mills
Richard Cane	St. Wolstans
Richard Maunsell	Oakley Park

the vestry for re-sale. It was recorded that in 1824 £630 was still due to the Board of First Fruits and that it was expected to have the loan repaid in full by 1849.[51] This estimate of thirty-six years to repay the loan differs greatly from the 1813 estimate of sixteen years and it would seem to indicate an over-optimistic approach to the original select vestry. Unfortunately there is in fact no record of when the loan was paid in full.

The annual vestry minutes record the agreement of planned expenditure for the parish for the coming year and these are minuted from 1825 to 1833.

Year	*Estimate of Expenditure*
1825	£71 8s. 0d.
1826	£72 0s. 0d.
1827	£101 0s. 0d.
1828	£90 11s. 3d.
1829	£56 6s. 0d.
1830	£78 6s. 7d.
1831	£15 4s. 7d.
1832	£55 11s. 2d.
1833	£52 0s. 0d.

The divergence in these estimates can be explained after analysis – for example the increase in 1827 is due to a bill for slating the church of £30. The low-estimate for 1831 is because of a surplus accrued from previous years. After 1829 the planned expenditure is clearly divided into two sections – first expenditure on charity which as already mentioned seemed like a civil obligation on the established church:

1830 expenditure on charity[52]

Coffins for the poor	...	£3
For the welfare of foundlings		
(orphans or abandoned children)	...	£ 5 5s. 0d.
To vestry clerk and applotte	...	£ 9 4s. 7d.
	Total	£17 9s. 7d.

The second part of the estimated expenditure related strictly to church business e.g. 1830

Payment to First Fruits	...	£9 4s. 7d.
Payment to Parish Clerk	...	£9 4s. 7d.
Payment to Sextoness	...	£9 4s. 7d.
Sacramental Elements	...	£3 3s. 10d.
Sweeping, turf, candles	...	£4 6s. 10d.
Washing of Surplus	...	£1 0s. 1d.
Repair of Slates	...	£1 0s. 1d.
	Total	£38 6s. 27d.

This sum of money to pay for parish expenditure would then be raised by the collection of tithes (taxes) from all of the landed inhabitants of the parish by collectors (proctors) who were paid one shilling for every pound collected. The setting of planned expenditure and the addition of payment to the proctors was called the applotment. For most years between 1825 and 1833 the tithe applotment was in the region of £50 to £80. In 1826, as already remarked, because of the necessity to repair the church roof the applotment soared to £101.

The natural resentment felt by any Catholic landholders at paying tithes must certainly have increased when faced with this increase. The following year the applotment was back down to £63 but the church wardens would not sign the accounts as all of the previous cess had not been collected.[53] In response to the general agitation against tithes, the Parliament passed a number of tithe composition acts in the 1820s.[54] These bills were designed to encourage the tithe payers of each parish to settle on a fixed amount of money which could be paid annually for a period of twenty one years. This it was hoped would remove the erratic nature of the tithes and would also remove the necessity of employing the much-hated proctor or tithe-collector. The select vestry held special meetings when requested to do so by the tithe-payers of the different parishes who financially supported the incumbent of Kildrought.

A figure of £190 sterling to be paid annually by the parishioners of Donacomper[55] was agreed on 27 July 1828, £145 sterling by the parishioners of Kildrought[56] which was agreed on 14 June 1830 and £100 sterling as an annual compensation for all the tithes of the said parish of Killadoon[57] was agreed on 2 August 1831. The two additional parishes mentioned here, Donacomper and Killadoon, had no separate 'church vestry or place of worship'[58] but were all served by the vicar and church of Kildrought. It must also be noted that the total tithe composition of £430 annually was to pay also for the salary of vicar and curate (which were estimated in 1869 as being £250 and £50 respectively per year).[59] This was indeed a substantial income for the time and also as the initiative for composition had come from the parishioners themselves (Catholic and Church of Ireland) it was now much more likely to be paid. Under an act of Parliament which received royal assent on 15 August 1838 – 'tithes and tithe compositions were abolished and replaced by a rent charge equal to seventy five per cent of the nominal value of the tithes. Responsibility for payment of this fee rested with the landlord, not the tenant'.[60] In future the payments to the local incumbent were incorporated into the tenants rent which he was to pay to his landlord and so much of the friction, between the Church of Ireland and the peasantry, was removed.

There are no further accounts recorded in the vestry minute books after 1833 until 1870. It is interesting to note however the list of charges to be placed by the church on its services as agreed by the select vestry on 14 June 1825. It is interesting to note the different value placed on different services and the insight this gives us into life at the time.

For breaking ground for burial in churchyard	...	£0 2s. 2d.
For a velvet pall on entering the church	...	£0 19s. 6d.
For a black plush or velvet pall	...	£0 7s. 7d.
For a flatstone in church yard	...	£8 0s. 0d.
For a headstone in church yard	...	£2 0s. 0d.
For churching of women	...	£0 2s. 8d.
For ringing bell at time of death	...	6d.

There was in fact a long list of services which the church was willing to provide but all at a cost.[61] Is this a further indication as in the case of the delay in making full repayment of the loan to the Board of First Fruits, that finances are in short supply. The Poor Book and the Holy Communion Book covering the years 1846 until 1860 show that the church even after the removal of tithes continued in its role of caring for the poor of the parish.

The Act of Disestablishment of the Church of Ireland,[62] which came into force on 1 January 1871, was a tremendous challenge to the parish's finances as the church was to take 'its place among all the denominations in Ireland as

self-supporting. Everything save the annuities secured by the existing clergy
and church officers has to be provided for by the Protestant owners of property
and by the accustomed members of congregation in each parish.'[63] When we
consider that the small number of parishioners was in decline from 294[64] in
1881 to 200[65] in 1900, it is obvious that a change of outlook and remarkable
generosity were being requested by each parishioner. A professional approach
was taken to this challenge and each year four accounts were prepared for the
inspection of parishioners:

1. General Sustentation Fund to make provision for future rectors and curates.
2. Charity Sermons Account showing the finances raised for such groups as
   the Protestant Orphan Society and the Irish Church Missions.
3. Account number three dealt with funds lodged with the Representative
   Church Body and held by them in trust for Celbridge parish.
4. Account of Sunday Collections which provided for the expenses of the
   parish such as insurance, fuel, lighting, rent of Curates house, etc.

Account number one, which was to provide for future vicars and curates had
£228 paid into it annually in the years in which the parish ledger accounts are
available. Account number one shows the amount collected in the church for
various charities after a sermon was preached and these collections were usually paid immediately to the charity in question. Money collected each year
for account number three was held in trust and parts of it used annually to
supplement accounts one and four covered the general expenses of the parish.

Based on an analysis of these accounts from 1871 to 1882,[66] the only years
for which they are available, the following abbreviated table gives an indication of annual parish expenses. In brackets in column four I have indicated the
sums used for charity in the parish.

Year	A/C No. 1 To Sustentation Fund (amounts paid into)	A/C No. 2 to Charity Sermons Fund	A/C No. 3 Funds held in Trust	A/C No. 4 To Parish Expenses	
1872	£228	£22	£32	£95	(£33)
1873	£228	£10	£31	£84	(£33)
1874	£228	£28	£31	£104	(£33)
1875	£228	£22	£29	£92	(£33)
1876	£228	£38 1s. 0d.	£29	£101 11s. 8d.	(£25)

It should be noted that the figures in the Sustentation account were the
sums which the parish had to pay but in some cases the funds collected had

to be augmented by sums of £20 and £30 transferred from account number three, designated for funds held in trust for just such an eventuality. There is no great difference between the amount required by the parish to fulfil its obligations for 1871 to 1881. In that year two new accounts were opened – account number five for the purchase of a glebe house for the rector and account number six for the establishment of a parochial school. However, when we consider that sums in the region of £400 to £500 had to be raised each year in the parish from a diminishing congregation it was indeed a considerable challenge. The burden was only able to be carried thanks to the wealth and generosity of a small number of parishioners. Two very generous contributions are worthy of note – Thomas Conolly's donation of £1,000 to the central fund in July of 1870[67] and Joseph Shaw's payment of £1,000 in 1882[68] towards the restoration of the church.

The following figures are abstracted from parish surveys recorded in the Preacher's books for the years 1880 to 1900. These surveys are all dated 30 June and relate to the year ending at that date. [69] They are recorded as visitation records and presumably they were for presentation to a member of the hierarchy.

Year Ending	Members of church in parish	Average Sunday Morning Congregation	Average Sunday School	Total of all funds collected in parish
30/6/1881	294	129	24	£851 16s. 0d.
30/6/1886	290	135	26	£999 10s. 8d.
30/6/1891	220	132	24	£837 0s. 9d.
30/6/1896	200	118	22	£304 0s. 1d.
30/6/1890	200	110	19	£294 13s. 3d.
Total drop in period	−94	−19	−5	−£557 2s. 9d.

These figures illustrate clearly the decline in the parish numbers mentioned elsewhere in this chapter. The big drop in funds collected in the parish relates to the fact that the collections for the Glebe house ceased in 1890. In that year Celbridge Lodge, former home of Shaw the millowner, was purchased by the parish as a glebe house for the rector for the sum of £1,116 6s. 8d.[70] One cannot mistake however the overall features of decline and with the total annual income now at £294 13s. 3d. at the end of the century it would seem to indicate that the parish would have difficulty in meeting its financial requirements. The positive side of course was that the parochial school would now have been funded largely by the National Board of Education (taken in charge 1889)[71] and the church had been renovated at a cost of £2616 in 1885.[72]

The finances of the Church of Ireland are a complex issue and I have attempted only to indicate the hurdles which had to be overcome. In the early years up until 1838 the church was funded by tithes collected from all landed parishioners including Catholics. This was later changed under the tithe composition acts but the effect was still that the people in the parish with land were financially supporting the Established Church. It must be admitted that the church seems to have had certain obligations going with this position such as making provision for the poor. Disestablishment offered a challenge to the members of the Church of Ireland to be independent financially. The initial response to this was positive but at the century's end the financial omens were bad.

EDUCATION

The first official information available on the education of Protestants is to be found in the 1826 Royal Commission of Irish Education Inquiry.[73] It listed ten fee paying schools in the parish and in four of these there were Protestants attending. The table below is an abbreviation of the Inquiry's findings.

Name of Teacher	Teacher's Religion	Description of school	Average no. of Protestants Attending
Edward Williams	Protestant	Vestry Room of Church	18
Catherine Williams	Protestant	Room in house	3
Michael Daly	Roman Catholic	House made of lime and stone	10
Rachel Bradish	Protestant	Held in part of house	24

Additional information regarding funding of these schools shows that Edward Williams' school was supported by the vicar who paid £2 annually and it also collected £24 in fees from parents. Catherine Williams' school survived on £8 collected annually from parents. Rachel Bradish and Michael Daly's schools shared the school house built by Lady Louisa Conolly and each teacher received a payment of £20 annually from Colonel Conolly. All four of these schools also catered for Catholics and in all four schools the authorised (Established Church) version of the Scriptures were read. The Conolly family's benevolent involvement in education dated back to Speaker Conolly's planning of the school later known as Celbridge Charter School. In 1814 Lady Louisa Conolly had opened a school at Castletown gates beside the newly erected church where education was provided free. It was originally intended to be a school for Protestants only but when she realised that Catholics were also in attendance she was overjoyed.[74] She later (1820) opened a School of Industry to educate and employ children of both denominations. Religious instruction was given one day a week in separate rooms by their own clergyman. The school was the first of its kind in Ireland and was co-educational. In 1821 thirty pupils attended, the boys were taught carpentry, tailoring, shoe-making and basket making. The girls were shown how to knit, sew and plait straw for making bonnets.

The tradition of mixed denominational schooling would seem to have continued and the church does not seem to have involved itself to any great degree in the education of its parishioners. The only mention of education in the select vestry minutes occurs in the Easter vestry minutes of 1866[75] when it has been agreed to collect funds from certain parishioners which would be spent on the cleaning and maintenance of the school – presumably this refers to the school operating from the vestry rooms of the church. This school seems to have been encountering difficulties however, as the select vestry minutes of 23 April 1878 record the passing of a motion expressing the desirability of maintaining a Parochial school in Celbridge and the necessity of raising funds in aid of this object.[76] Their efforts must have failed however as the vestry minutes of 12 January 1880 record 'seeing that the town of Celbridge is at present without any school for poor Protestants, save as are conducted by Roman Catholics, steps must be taken to open such a school'.[77] It would seem that the complacency towards multi-denominational education had gone.

In 1881 this school was established, in the premises of what had been Lady Louisa's school of industry, after agreeing a payment of £50 per annum to Mr. Conolly.[78] Parishioners and parents had to finance this school on their own because as Akenson says, referring to the years up until the late 1860s – 'the Church of Ireland refused to have anything to do with the national system of education. Indeed they treated it as a product of the devil rather than as a convenient source of government funds'.[79] To the cost of rental of the building had to be added the teachers payment of '£50 per annum together with house and garden free and two tons of coal per annum'.[80] This payment also entailed playing the church organ on Sundays.

By 1887 however the select vestry were anxious to put the school under the National Board of Education. An application to the Commissioners of National Education for the payment of a teachers salary and the supply of requisites is attached to a detailed profile of the school.[81] The school is described as being located close to Christ Church, Celbridge in a large school building, high and lofty, divided in two by a removable partition. The teacher's accommodation was at one end of the partition.

It seems that the £50 yearly rental on the premises had gone and it was given to the select vestry free of rent.[82] The school operates from 10 am until

3pm with religious instruction at 11 o'clock for thirty minutes each day. The reasons for the application were given as – 'subscriptions have been diminishing through death and other causes and the need is felt for a more thorough inspection of the school than is possible under the Diocesan system'.[83] Another application followed in 1888[84] praising the qualities of the teacher Miss Keegan and declaring that the teacher prior to her was actually a recognised national school teacher and had only been dismissed 'as she was unable to play the organ in church'.[85] Though the school had been conducted since its foundation in 1881 according to the Board of Education principles, it failed to get Board approval because the teacher Miss Keegan, did not have the necessary qualifications. The Board however would make no exceptions and Miss Keegan was let go and a qualified teacher was employed.[86] Eventually, having checked that the managers of the existing Board had no objections (Fr. Donovan of the Abbey National schools and the Clerk of the Union Workhouse schools) the school was finally accepted by the Board.[87] The number of children on the school roll books was thirty-two in 1891[88] and twenty-four by 1900.[89]

In retrospect it seems surprising that the Church of Ireland was so casual in the provision of a solely Protestant school and subsequently in bringing their school established in 1881 under the direct control and financing of the National Board of Education. It is noteworthy that when the final and successful application to the Board was made in 1889, Charles Graham had to state that the school would be open to all denominations and state the specific daily time of religious instruction. As we have seen in the section dealing with the provision of education for Catholics, the reputedly non-denominational nature of the national school system in Celbridge toward the century's end, was what might now be called 'an Irish solution to an Irish problem'.

In 1729 Speaker Conolly set up a school for forty poor children, to educate and to instruct them in useful occupations.[90] It became known as Celbridge Charter or Collegiate school and it was located about a mile from Celbridge town on the Clane road. He provided an elaborate building as premises and provided finance for its future development. By the beginning of the nineteenth century it had become a girls only school and in 1811 Lady Louisa Conolly had it transferred to the control of the Incorporated Society in Dublin for promoting English Protestant Schools in Ireland. We may presume that she saw in this the best future for the school. The move is difficult to understand, considering her previous liberal approach towards respecting the religious integrity of Catholics. Under the terms of the agreement the Conolly family would pay £250 and annuities of £50 if they were allowed to nominate up to thirty children for placement in the school.[91] Of the first thirty six nominated to the school, twenty four were Catholic and twelve were Protestant. All of Lady Louisa's nominees were from Celbridge.[92] The Incorporated Society nominated only Protestant girls and according to the Royal Commission of Enquiry issued in 1826[93] there were 126 – all Protestants.

As can be seen from the figure below Catholics were soon excluded or perhaps excluded themselves from the school.

Year	Total No of Pupils	Catholics	Protestants
1810[94]	111	63	48
1826	126	0	126

It is also of interest to examine the religious persuasion of new entrants to the college as recorded for the three years below.[95]

Year	Total	Catholic	Protestant	Of mixed parents
1835	14	1	10	3
1836	17	1	14	2
1837	7	–	6	1

This issue of children of a marriage where the parents are of a different religious persuasion is one that almost goes unmentioned in nineteenth century documentation. The Incorporated Society would seem to have been anxious to educate and perhaps influence such children. This would seem to contradict Speaker Conolly's will which sought merely to educate poor children and to instruct them in useful occupations.[96]

The local committee which managed the affairs of the school included Edward Conolly, the earl of Leitrim, Lord Cloncurry and Arthur Henry of Lodge Park – the elite of the Church of Ireland gentry.[97] The minutes of their meetings recorded the day to day affairs of the school but also occasionally betray opinions we might consider unusual – 'We continued in our opinion as to the propriety of habituating all the female children to early practices of neatness and consider the want of night-caps a remarkable deficiency'.[98] Though no mention of religion appeared in the minutes of these meetings it is obvious from the report of the deputation of the Incorporated Society which visited the school in 1848[99] that it was high on the schools agenda. 'The business of the day commenced with a prayer conducted by the Catechist Mr. Greer ... The subjects for examination were Holy Scripture, the Church Catechism, Reading, Writing and Spelling'. The report of the 1849 deputation recorded that of the fifty six girls in the school, twenty seven were Conolly nominees. At the time of the visitation an examination was held of children from Protestant schools in the country who sought admission. It is obvious from their comments that it was a charity school and not the place where children of the better off would be educated – 'It is a painful fact that one of the successful candidates is a daughter of a deceased clergyman of the Established

Church. The distressed state of his family render her admission as a matter of importance'.[100]

In the 1880s a long legal dispute took place between the Conolly family and the Incorporated Society regarding the £394 which the family paid annually for its right to have thirty nominees in the school.[101] Letters written by Mrs. Conolly at the time show that while the average cost of maintenance, clothing and educating of a girl in any of several institutions surveyed at the time was between £10 and £15, the cost for the same in the charter school was £25.[102] One of Mrs. Conolly's solutions to this problem was that all girls sponsored by the Conolly foundation should be made do all of the housework which, while cutting down on the schools expenses, would also prepare the girls for any situation which they might be required to fill. Eventually the dispute between the Conolly family and the Incorporated Society was brought to a close when legal opinion delivered in 1890 declared that the original agreement between the two parties was wholly irregular. It would seem that the Conolly family's involvement in the school ended at that time. The school continued however to operate as a girls boarding school, though in different form, up until 1972.

The Church of Ireland in Celbridge was a small community and a study of the baptism figures and the school and parish records show that the school population was declining for the second half of the century. It is very unlikely that the children of the wealthy landowners attended these fee-paying schools in the village and this may explain the casual approach adopted by the select vestry to the schools situation until disestablishment when the growing monopoly of the Catholic Church in the schools, prompted the vestry into establishing a proper parish school. The Conolly family seem to have had a genuine concern for the education of poor children of all creeds but under the Incorporated Society, the Collegiate school gradually became an almost totally Protestant school for the less well-off girls. As the Catholic Church emerged from its penal days seclusion, it would seem, that the Church of Ireland, sensing a demographic threat, began slowly to nurture its own separate schooling system.

ROLE IN SOCIETY

Until 1869 the Church of Ireland did not have to struggle to maintain its supreme position in the parish – it was after all the established church of the state. An analysis of its receipts column for the 1847 accounts shows that it was even the recipient of fines levied at the local court of petty sessions.[103] In fact as I have already mentioned earlier the select vestry had in fact what seems to have been almost certain civil duties and responsibilities for the poor prior to the setting up of the workhouses in 1838.

A study of the church papers show also however, that it did take seriously
its responsibilities to the poor of the parish. Two sets of accounts are of particular value – the Celbridge Poor Accounts 1846–1860 and the Holy Communion
Book 1846–1860. The Poor Accounts record the weekly collections made for
the poor, often naming generous contributors and detailing how the money
was spent. This table summarises a part of the annual returns which are available from these accounts.[104]

Year	Receipts	Expenditure	Balance
1846	£99 17s. 11d.	£96 3s. 4d.	£3 14s. 7d.
1847	£84 2s. 5d.	£70 5s. 6d.	£13 16s. 11d.
1848	£82 9s. 3d.	£82 3s. 5d.	£0 5s. 11d.
1849	£115 4s. 9d.	£107 14s. 0d.	£7 11s. 91d.

These figures would seem to corroborate the opinion that the famine was not
very severe in the parish, as the rector would hardly have allowed a balance to
remain in his account, if the situation was desperate. It is worthwhile to con-
trast these figures for the famine years with the figures of a decade later.

Year	Receipts	Expenditure	Balance
1856	£75 18s. 3d.	£69 12s. 7d.	£6 5s. 8d.
1857	£67 11s. 2d.	£68 0s. 10d.	- £0 9s. 8d.
1858	£67 10s. 8d.	£62 6s. 5d.	£4 13s. 1d.
1859	£70 3s. 1d.	£66 14s. 3d.	£3 9s. 8d.

Although all of these figures of receipts and expenditure are lower, the figures
of the famine years are not that substantially greater to indicate a major and
urgent demand for relief. In fact the expenditure on relief of the poor only
differs by slightly over £2 between 1847 and 1857. Of the fifteen years recorded,
in only two years did expenditure exceed receipts – 1855 and 1857. 1855 was
also the year of highest receipts and expenditure and would seem to indicate
a difficult year for the poor in the parish. This is corroborated by the remarks
of the Rev. Packenham in the side columns of the book in January. 'During
the late intensely severe frost and snow, the following donations were received
for the general distribution among the poor for food, fuel and clothing ...'.[105]
The charity does seem to have been distributed among the poor regardless of
creed. This conclusion is based on the evidence of the surnames of recipients
such as Doyle, O'Grady, Farrell, O'Dea. These surnames do not occur in the
Protestant parish registers but are common in the Catholic registers. Indeed
specific mention is made on occasions when the recipient is Protestant e.g.

'April 29th 1859 to a poor Protestant named McRoy, a soldier's wife to assist her in her journey home'.[106]

The money from this account was in fact expended in many different ways, for example the provision of coffins and graves for the poor and the provision of beef. The money we must assume was collected at the weekly church service and it was dispensed by the kindly Robert Pakenham (vicar 1829–1881) who usually signed his accounts in the following manner – 'I have distributed all the annexed contributions among the suffering poor'.[107]

The Holy Communion books would seem to have been a record of support given strictly to poor Protestants. The amounts collected and dispensed are much smaller – usually £20 and £30 annually. Again the surnames such as Grundy, Thompson, Dobson and Lumley would seem to indicate Protestant recipients and also comments such as 'To repair shoes so that the poor children can attend evening meetings for scripture reading'.[108] It would seem that these specific funds were available for those poor Protestants who had received Holy Communion on that Sunday. This table lists the annual figures for this account covering the same years as shown in the table for the Poor Accounts.[109]

Holy Communion Book Accounts (Recorded to the nearest pound)

Year	Receipts	Expenditure	Balance
1846	£25	£21	£4
1847	£29	£26	£3
1848	£22	£19	£3
1849	£23	£18	£5
1856	£31	£31	–
1857	£25	£23	£2
1858	£27	£27	–
1859	£28	£20	£8

As can be seen by these figures they are considerably less than the annual figures from the Poor Accounts perhaps because there was less need in this area. It is evident also that Rev. Packenham tries to err on the side of caution when balancing his books.

Evidence of the important role that the rector was seen to have had in an area can be found in the communications between the Relief Commission and the Rev. Packenham at the time of the famine.[110] In one of his replies to the Commissioners Packenham promises 'I will use my best exertions to allay excitement in the parish occasioned by the failure of the potato crop'.

That individual members of the Church of Ireland held important positions in the administration of the town is certain – all members of grand juries, justices for the peace and Boards of Guardians were Protestant until after

1850. I have already demonstrated the illustrious composition of the men who formed the select vestry. But there were many poor people who were Protestants as we have seen in our analysis of the expenditure of the Holy Communion book. To try to ascertain the actual social make up of the Church of Ireland community I have examined the returns for the census of 1901 – the first census to provide all the data necessary.[111] 166 people can be identified who specified their religion as being Church of Ireland. The break-down of their professions (occupations) is as follows:

Child (student)	...	47
Retired	...	5
Mother/Housewife	...	19
Farm Labourer or Gardener	...	23
Domestic Servant	...	38
Unemployed	...	3
Self-employed	...	9
Gentlemen/Farmers	...	8
Professionals	...	6
No answer	...	8
Total		166

If we exclude children, housewives, those retired, unemployed and those who gave no answer from the total figure we get a figure of eighty-four between the remaining occupations.

Total figure	...	166
–Children/Housewives/Retired	...	–82
Unemployed/No answer	...	
All other occupations	=	84

Of these eighty-four a total of sixty-one people were employed as either gardeners, farm labourers or domestic servants. It becomes very evident from any analysis of the census that the Protestant families were in fact grouped mainly in the vicinity of the large houses such as Castletown and Kiladoon. It seems that the wealthy Protestant landowners did consciously employ Protestants where possible in their houses and on their farms. It is also noticeable how few (three) are identified as unemployed.

From this analysis I must conclude that in fact the power and wealth that was associated with this small community, that was the Church of Ireland, was in fact confined to a small elite group within the church – the Conolly's,

Maunsell's, Cane's, Clement's and Shaw's. In the decades prior to disestablishment the church, through its vicar and select vestry, did command a certain amount of authority because of its established position. After disestablishment this power waned as can be seen by its many futile attempts to have the school taken under the auspices of the National Board of Education. Despite all of this however, because the important power brokers in the parish were nearly all Protestant, the Church of Ireland was seen to carry an influence in society far in excess of what its population would have merited, right to the end of the century.

CONCLUSION

As mentioned at the beginning of this chapter, the formal nature of the Church of Ireland papers make it very difficult to obtain a personal insight into the vicars of the parish. Robert Packenham seems to have been a strong and respected character who kept a steady hand on the wheel of his church as it negotiated its way through the fifty three years (1829 to 1881) that he was vicar of Kildrought. His name is never connected with controversy but is only mentioned in the performance of his duties to church and parish. Charles Graham (vicar 1881 to 1911) oversaw the restoration of a parish school in 1891, and guided this school towards the recognition by the National Board of Education in 1889. They were men who lived through difficult times but they have left their imprint on their parish that is still visible to this day.

To the small Church of Ireland community in Celbridge, the nineteenth century was a period of great change. After the Tithe Acts and the Act of Disestablishment it had to learn to stand on its own feet. Though its numbers were in decline it certainly reacted enthusiastically to its changed circumstances. Perhaps it was the democratic and open nature of its organisation which enabled it to grasp the extent to which its circumstances had changed and to respond in such an effective manner to these changes?

Within the Church of Ireland community there was a smaller community who held most of the wealth and power in the parish. This group had an inordinate amount of input and influence into the parish's development. Their wealth and generosity were vital to the church. As an institution in the parish it finished the century in a weaker position than at the century's start. As an organisation of Protestant believers it saw the century out as a leaner, more independent, democratic and effective force.

Co-operation and Conflict

It is difficult to appraise with certainty the true nature of the relationship between the two religious groupings in the parish. In a small community, such as Celbridge, there would have been a great deal of interdependence and so if there were undercurrents of hostility they would not tend to surface in written form. This was particularly noticeable in the Church of Ireland papers which tended to be formal records and open to public inspection to some degree. The letters from the Catholic Church papers were in the main private and so we are more likely to glimpse from them what was really happening in the parish.

As seen in previous chapters it was a period of great change in the parish. The census figures do not give a breakdown of population figures along denominational lines until 1861, so that a comparison of the church registers will give us the clearest understanding of the demographic trends available. A comparison of baptisms registered shows (Figure 7) a decline in both churches from 1830 onwards. The decline of the Catholic baptisms is, from a peak of 1,203 for the period 1821 to 1830, to a low of 507 for the period 1881 to 1890. The period 1891 to 1900 records an increase of Catholic registered baptisms to 523. The peak period for Church of Ireland baptisms was 1811–1820 when 188 were recorded but from that time on there was a constant decline until only twenty nine were registered for the years 1891–1900. This certainly did not bode well for the church's future. A comparison of the marriage figures (Figure 8) shows a peak period for marriages in the middle decades when the mills were at their peak. The decline of Catholic marriages registered is quite dramatic but the Church of Ireland figures remain low but constant. The ratio of baptisms to marriages registered in the Catholic church is 4.9:1 and in the Church of Ireland it is 4.6:1. All of these figures show a parish in demographic decline but with Catholic baptisms outnumbering Church of Ireland baptisms by 18:1 for the period 1891–1900. If we compare this with the 1821–1830 figure of 6.7:1 we can understand why the Church of Ireland may have felt threatened.

The indications of co-operation and friendship between both groups will be considered first. Individual families and people seem to have cultivated good relations between both denominations. The Conolly family provided the site or the Catholic church free of rent.[1] Lady Louisa Conolly purposely provided non-denominational education free in the village and as she said – 'pleased myself with the thought that I had Catholics and Protestants all mixed

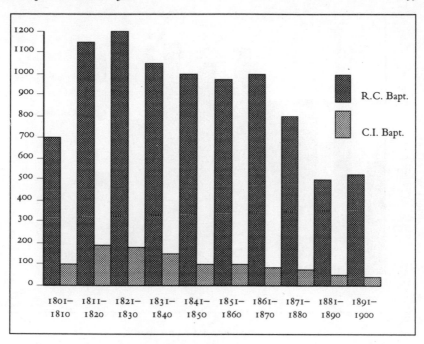

7. Comparison of Baptisms

up as they should be and growing up together in their childhood, in all probability will make them grow up with cordiality towards each other'.[2] Affection and respect for Lady Louisa was universal in the village according to a letter of sympathy[3] sent by the parish priest James Callanan and his parishioners to the Conolly family after her death in October 1821 – 'In her the poor have lost a comforter and protector ... her kindness particularly to the poor of our persuasion shall never be erased from our memories'.[4] They went on to praise her school of industry at Castletown Gates – 'securing thereby the blessings of education unalloyed by any interference or distinction of religion to the children of this poor and populous district'.[5]

According to the Education Survey of 1826[6] the majority of schools were in fact catering for children of mixed religions and this would seem to have continued throughout the century until the demographic decline of the Church of Ireland left most of the schools entirely Catholic, except for the vestry school which catered strictly for Protestants.

Further evidence of goodwill was seen in the contributions made to the new Catholic church by the Kirkpatrick family.[7] The Poor Accounts[8] as already mentioned in the last chapter detailed the collections made and the subsequent distributions of funds by the rector to the poor of the town, irrespective of religion.

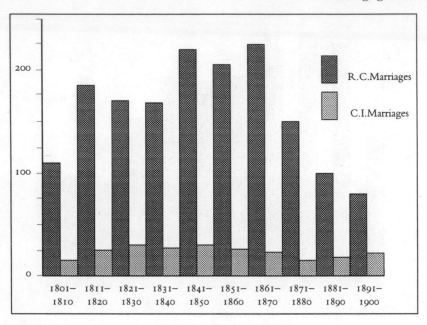

8. Comparison of Marriages

Despite these individual examples of co-operation it is inevitable that there would have been bitterness on the Catholic side caused by the sheer injustice of the situation. This anger and suspicion can be found in a number of letters and reports. The earliest Parish Report[9] of 1820 consists of a count of the number of Catholic houses (thirty-two)) and the House of Sectaries (non-Catholic) (forty). The terminology betrays a suspicion and demonstrates a Catholic hierarchy which is assessing its superiority of numbers. The 1834 Report[10] was an even more detailed census of the denominations, including a breakdown of ages and gender. But most interesting of all is the assessment of Catholic males (thirty-one) and Catholic females (sixty-five) in Protestant employment. This betrays a suspicion of proselytising by the Protestant employers. This same suspicion surfaced in a letter of complaint[11] against Fr. Murphy P.P. in 1834 which deplored the fact that he had made no provision for the Catholic schools – 'while the enemies of our holy religion are holding contrary inducements to pervert the souls of Catholics'.[12] A letter of complaint against his parish priest by curate Patrick Woods in 1844 listed the deplorable state of the church building but we can see his anger and humiliation when he added in a postscript to his letter – 'Very lately the Rev. Mr. Packenham, Rector of the parish, stopped me on the street to draw my attention to this matter'.[13] An element of resentment towards the proposed new Catholic church building can be glimpsed when in October 1854 a curate Fr. Lynch wrote to the archbishop recommending that a site be purchased – 'There is adjoining the chapel grounds what is called Brewery Yard – containing 2 acres with building materials being most eligible for a convent and chapel to be had at very reasonable terms if applied *for by a lay party*.'[14] Rev. Lynch may have been worried that the owners of the property would not be willing to sell (or would seek an excessive price for) the ground if they knew it was to have a Catholic church built on it. He hoped to circumvent this problem by suggesting that a lay person would purchase the land for the church.

One of the strongest indications of mistrust between the two churches is the 1854 letter of Fr. Lynch to Archbishop Cullen in which he listed the 'perverts' (the opposite of convert, people who left the Catholic church and turned to Protestantism) of the parish.[15] He listed their names and the number of children in their family. After that he added a list of observations of each person, for instance, 'Thomas Magee a carpenter who is in the employment of Shaw who keeps a proselytising school, Mary Neil a servant in the ministers employment'.[16] He seems to have had a great dislike and distrust of Shaw, the mill-owner but some of his other observations are even more damning – 'Bridget White-Prostitute, living with another's husband, Charley Smyth – father of the highway man shot by the police in Celbridge some months ago'.[17] There would even seem to have been some profit to be gained by conversion – 'Markee and Wife – were some time ago converts from Protestantism, considered to make traffic in religion'.[18] He listed a total of seventy-three people whom he believed had deserted Catholicism for Protestantism and if his figures are even near to being correct we can understand the mistrust, even enmity which this would lead to.

As already mentioned the papers of the Church of Ireland are of a more formal nature but nevertheless there are some extracts worth examining. The select vestry in 1884 took strong objection to the placing of 'the letters I.H.S. or other symbol of letters which might give offence to some parishioners over the porch or within the (new) church'.[19] These letters are of biblical significance meaning Jesus Christ Saviour and would be associated with the high church element of the Anglican church which was seen by some to have been closer in its practices to Catholicism. Many within the Church of Ireland would have rejected anything which could possibly be seen as leaning in this direction. Further evidence of this hostility is contained in the statement of the first general assembly of vestrymen after disestablishment on 4 July 1870. 'We take this opportunity to declare our hearty sympathy with and entire approval of, the expression of devoted attachment to the Bible and Protestant principles. This meeting desires to join in the general denunciation of all attempts to introduce ritualistic practices, unusual in the public services of the church'.

Whereas the Catholic population would have supported political change to various degrees, the select vestry minutes of 3 March 1893 record – 'We protest against the measure which has been introduced into the House of Commons under the title Government of Ireland Bill. We are convinced that if the revolutionary changes proposed were carried out it would seriously imperil the safeguards of civil and religious liberty and the integrity of the Great Empire of which the United Kingdom is the centre'.[20] But perhaps the single episode in the parish history of that time which reveals most of interdenominational relations and which received national media attention took place in the months of May and June 1861. The stage where this confrontation was to take place was Celbridge Workhouse and the leading characters were Mr. Wolfe (the master of the house), Mr. Lennen (the clerk) and Mrs. Dobson (the matron), all Protestants. The story begins when the master and the clerk were accused of inserting on the roll, the names of paupers who were not in existence. An officer of the Poor Law Commission was sent to Celbridge to investigate the matter and as Fr. Daniel Byrne said in his letter to Archbishop Cullen – 'when Mr. Wolfe was about to be sworn, the clerk objected saying he [Wolfe] did not believe in the existence of God. The charge was repeated against Wolfe by Mrs. Dobson in a letter subsequently delivered to the Board of Guardians. Mrs. Dobson, the matron in consequence of charges made against her was also called upon to resign'.[21]

The investigating committee failed to establish any case of gross impropriety on the part of the matron but they were of the opinion that her conduct had been such as to render it desirable that she should resign. Mr. Maunsell, vice-chairman of the Board of Guardians, after consultation with his superiors in the Poor Law Commission, discovered that if the Board of Guardians voted to retain her this would be acceptable. A furious Fr. Byrne, (P.P. 1855 to 1865) continued in his letter to Archbishop Cullen 'In a Board of Guardians in which out of 30 only 13 are Catholic, a majority was easily secured. On this occasion several guardians attended who scarcely ever take part. I may as well mention that Mr. Wolfe, Mr. Lennen and Mrs. Dobson all belong to the established church, the inmates being mainly Catholic, there not being 20 Protestants in the house out of a total of 280'.

The scene next shifted to London where Archbishop Cullen was addressing the Irish Poor Relief Commission on May 28 1861. Cullen despised the workhouse system and he hoped to use this opportunity to bring it into disrepute. 'I bring to your notice a very painful case which was brought to my notice some time since. Mr. Wolfe the Master of Celbridge Workhouse, discovered a poor woman in the act of bringing out bread from her own dinner to give to her daughter. He took it from her and threw it to a pig'.[22] He went on to relate the story of the dismissals, the atheism of the master and the interference of the Board of Guardians in the recommended dismissal of the Matron – 'on the grounds that she had been improperly intimate with the Clerk'.[23]

The resentment of the Catholic church seems to have had a number of obvious causes such as the employment of Protestants and atheists to supervised vulnerable poor Catholics. Fr. Byrne however was also concerned for the morals of the women inmates when he referred not only to the matron but also to ten assistant or deputy nurses, some of whom had illegitimate children and some of them as many as three. The placing of such women in charge of the sick both male and female I already considered a great grievance ...[24]

The next part of this drama unfolded in the pages of the *Dublin Evening Mail*. Richard Maunsell, the deputy chairman of the Board of Guardians, who had helped to avoid the dismissal of the matron writes as follows – 'Sir, as you have published Dr. Cullen's evidence in respect to Celbridge Workhouse, may I ask you to insert the enclosed letter.'[25] Angrily he attacked the archbishop's evidence 'upon which he appears to have been entirely misinformed. No statement can be more mischievous or unjust than those partly true and partly false such as those which his Grace – no doubt with perfect innocence – has been the means of circulating'.[26] He continued to defend the matron with vigour 'and the single fact upon which the archbishop has been instructed to put forward – the cruel and unfounded charge that she had maintained an improper intimacy with the clerk – a charge which might ruin any lady of the highest rank – is this that the clerk had addressed to her by letter an honourable proposal of marriage which proposal the matron at once declined'.[27] He denied any interference by himself in the correct conduct of the affairs and attacked 'any person who may have informed the Rev. Daniel Byrne, who again informed Archbishop Cullen who again informed the Poor Law Inquiry'[28] that he, the deputy chairman had interfered. Lest anyone should consider the actions of Celbridge Board of Guardians to have been sectarian he concluded 'I beg to state that upon the last occasion when a vacancy for a school mistress arose a Roman Catholic was elected'.[29]

Some days later Charles Langdale, the person referred to by Maunsell as 'the person who may have informed Daniel Byrne', and a member of the Board of Guardians replied to Maunsell's letter. He defended Archbishop Cullen's remarks about the matron saying that the investigating commissioners had stated that 'an amount of intimacy has been proved to have existed'.[30] But his strongest blow was aimed at Maunsell's self-congratulatory remarks regarding the hiring of a Catholic teacher. 'At that time there were forty-four children in school, two thirds of whom were orphans and all but four Catholics. I ventured to state this as a motive for electing a Catholic mistress who might be able to hear these poor motherless children recite their morning and night prayers but I was answered to the effect that this was the Chaplain's business'.[31] There can be no hiding of Langdale's pent-up resentment towards Maunsell's portrayal of Protestant benevolence as he completed his letter – 'The result was, as Mr. Maunsell states, the Catholic was elected, I believe by a majority of three, there being twelve or thirteen votes given to the Protestant candidate, who I may mention was no other than Miss Dobson, the present discredited Matron. It is also true that there are some Protestants to their honour be it spoken — who voted in the majority'.[32]

Fr. Byrne enclosed a cutting of this letter from the *Dublin Evening Mail* with a letter of his own to Archbishop Cullen in which he said — 'There is great excitement about the evidence and I am convinced that the liberal cause will gain by the revelations.We had a great day at the workhouse yesterday ... '[33] He went on triumphantly to describe the election of a Catholic master of the workhouse and then to refer to the religion of one of the orphan children. It was the custom to raise such children as Protestants unless a strong case could be made contrary to this. Fr. Byrne declared 'I was present and took part in the examination (of the child) which lasted for six hours. The case was most complete and the other party had not an inch of ground to stand on, although they fought it out to the last and were present in great numbers'.[34] Maunsel had one more letter to the *Dublin Evening Mail* in which he protested — 'I totally deny the insulting statement of Dr. Cullen that I interfered with the procedure ... I can see that plainly enough that this part of Dr. Cullen's evidence is aimed not at me but to damage the Poor Law Commissioners'.[35] Again he denied any sectarian motives — 'had not the unfortunate question of Protestant and Roman Catholic been dragged into this case, there would have been no division whatever upon the Board in respect to the Matron's case'.[36] He concluded — 'I have engaged in controversy with reluctance, I quit it without anger'.[37]

The episode does not reveal evidence of a total conflict situation between the two denominations. Rather there was a tremendous resentment and desire for democratic change among all Catholics. Meanwhile some Protestants saw these moves towards change as a detrimental trend and fought to retain the status quo. Nevertheless relations between individuals and the church bodies were in general good. Many of the people of the parish of both denominations had in fact been educated together. More would have worked together with people of the opposite faith. Outside the door of the Catholic church is a large Celtic cross erected to the memory of 'Sir Gerald Dease 1831—1903 — a man of stainless honour — erected by his numerous friends of all classes and all creeds'.[38] The sentiments thus expressed may well be more representative of the co-operative relationship which existed among the majority of the population. But above all it was a time of change and change did not happen without undercurrents of resentment which occasionally broke to the surface. Mrs. Dobson, the Protestant matron remained in her position for only one more year.[39]

Conclusion

At the end of the nineteenth century the population of the parish of Celbridge (1,045) was about half of what it had been at the beginning of the century. An examination of the church documents for the century leaves one with the sense of prevailing poverty which seems to have rested like a dark cloud over the heads of the majority of the population. But there had been changes.

The Catholic church at the beginning of the century held the allegiance of the majority of the population but emerging as it was from days of state disapproval if not persecution it was in disarray. At times one might suspect that many of these people knew they were Catholic but perhaps did not know what being a Catholic involved. The Church of Ireland adherents would seem to have been strengthened by the isolation of their minority status. They were also the church of the state, the people of power, though this power and wealth was in fact confined to a minority within their ranks.

The impetus for change came from outside. The parliament in London was to enact over the century legislation adopting a more favourable approach to Catholics, such as the Catholic Emancipation Act of 1828 and the disestablishment of the Church of Ireland in 1869. The result of this changing environment was that the Catholic church was to adopt a higher profile in the parish. Another outside agent of change seems to have been the Catholic hierarchy which encouraged the local church to advance its position in society by increasing the sophistication of its organisation. Other agents of change from within the Catholic church were dynamic clerics such as Daniel Byrne and concerned, educated, wealthy lay people such as Charles Langton. Within the parish of Celbridge there were Protestants who facilitated change by their benevolent and Christian approach to education such as the Conolly and Grattan families.

These slow steps of advancement for Catholics and their church could be seen as a gradual progress towards democracy in parish society. Not all within the Protestant community welcomed these changes. But the force for change from outside the parish made moves towards change within the parish inevitable. Within the parish the sheer size of the Protestant community and its continuing loss of numbers again facilitated the inevitable advancement of Catholics in the parish.

At the close of the nineteenth century the position was far from democratic, reflecting the less than democratic nature of society in the nation as a whole. But power seems to have shifted from the hands of the local Protestant landlords into the hands of government bodies such as the National Board of Education. At this stage Catholics in Celbridge expected and received equality of treatment with their Protestant neighbours. The Protestant community must have undergone a similar gradual change in outlook.

But behind these badges of religion were real people who in their different ways sought only to get closer to their God. This reality was often clouded over by the politics, financial problems and personality clashes of the society that was nineteenth-century Celbridge. I hope that the story of these people and their churches has in some way illuminated our understanding of Celbridge then and now.

Appendices

Register of Catholic Curates, Parish of Celbridge 1800–1900

1843–1844	James Whittle
1845–1853	Patrick Woods
1853–1856	James Lynch
1856–1859	John Wheeler
1859–1862	John Wheeler and Michael Gibney
1862–1864	John Wheeler and Thomas Langan
1864–1868	John Wheeler and Joseph Nolan
1868–1874	John Wheeler and William Hampson
1874–1882	William Hampson
1882–1884	J. Farrell
1884–1885	P. O'Donnell
1885–1890	M. Hogan
1890–1896	John Kennedy
1896–1900	James Dempsey

APPENDIX 2

Year	Population	R.C. Baptisms	C. of I. Baptisms	R. C. Marriages	C. of I. Marriages
1801–1810	–	705	106	109	14
1811–1820	–	1146	188	184	24
1821–1830	1949 (in 1821)	1203	178	171	31
1831–1840	2295 (in 1831)	1044	151	170	26
1841–1850	1559 (in 1841)	1004	98	219	29
1851–1860	2010 (in 1851)	972	97	205	26
1861–1870	1883 (in 1861)	1009	80	224	21
1871–1880	1745 (in 1871)	809	67	146	13
1881–1890	1220 (in 1881)	507	33	100	16
1891–1900	1945 (in 1891)	523	29	84	20

Notes

ABBREVIATIONS

N.A.   National Archives
N.L.I.   National Library of Ireland
R.C.B.L.   Representative Church Body Library
T.C.D.   Trinity College Dublin
G.O.   Genealogical Office
D.D.A.   Dublin Diocesan Archives
J.K.A.S.   *Journal of the Kildare Archeological Society*
N.B.E.P.   National Board of Education Papers
C.S.V.M.   Celbridge Select Vestry Minutes in R.C.B.L.
Rep. Nov.   *Reportorium Novum*

INTRODUCTION

1   Lena Boylan, 'The Conollys of Castletown, a family history', *Irish Georgian Society Bulletin*, XI, No. 4 (Oct–Dec 1968), p. 6.

2   Tony Doohan, *A history of Celbridge*, (Dublin, 1984), p. 35.

3   Charles Topham Bowden, *A tour through Ireland*, 1790 (Dublin, 1791), p. 72.

4   Richard Twiss, *Tour in Ireland, 1776–1779*, (3 vols London, 1780) iii, p. 19.

5   *The New Travellers Guide* (Dublin and London, 1819), p. 114.

6   William Wilson, *Post Chaise Companion or Travellers Directory*, (3rd ed, Dublin, 1803), p. 133.

7   Coquebert de Montbret, *Carnets de Voyage* mss., in Bibliothèque Nationale de Paris, (Nouv. acq. xxxiii).

8   Arthur Young, *A tour in Ireland 1775*, (3 vols London, 1780), iii, p. 19.

9   Lena Boylan, The mills of Kildrought, *Journal of the Kildare Archaeological Society*, xv (1971–76), p. 359.

10 William Mason, *An account of Ireland statistical and political, 1814–1819* (Dublin), p. 717.

11 National Archive 620/12/1567/1–3, The Rebellion Papers, Co. Kildare.

12 National Library of Ireland, 7/2/1800, List of persons who suffered loss in 1798 rebellion.

13 Boylan, 'The Conollys of Castletown', p. 30.

14 *The Pettigrew almanac 1840*, (Dublin, 1840), p. 218.

15 George Taylor, Andrew Skinner, *Maps of the roads of Ireland – surveyed 1777*, (Dublin and London, 1778).

16 Major Alex Taylor, 'A Map of the County Kildare' in Thomas James Rawson's *Statistical Survey of Co. Kildare* (Dublin 1807).

17 Abstract of Answers and Returns of population in Ireland. HC 1833 (23) xxxix, 94–95.

18 Celbridge R.C. church, Marriage Register, Parish or Celbridge, 1854–1866.

19 *The Royal Commission on Education, Second Report 1826*, (Parochial Abstracts) HC 1826–7 (12) xii.i, p. 104

20 *Census of Ireland, Vol. II, Province of Leinster 1872*, (C.662) lxvii.i

21 Tony Doohan, *A History of Celbridge*.

22 Celbridge Library, *Celbridge Charter*, 1973 to 1995.

THE ROMAN CATHOLIC CHURCH

1 *Irish Catholic Directory*, 1836 to 1900 (65 vols) (Dublin), Parish of Celbridge.

2 D.D.A, Parish Report 1820, Murray file 31/2.

3 D.D.A Parish Report 1833, Murray file 31/4.

4 P.J. Corish, *The Irish Catholic Experience* (Dublin, 1985), p. 159.

5 *Irish Catholic Directory*, 1893, Clerical Register, Dublin Diocese, p. 106.

6 D.D.A., Census of the United Parishes of Celbridge and Straffan, 1834, Murray 31/4

7 *Abstract of Answers and returns of population in Ireland*, H.C, 1833 (23) xxxix, 94–95

8 D.D.A.,1839 Parish Report, Murray 31/7

9 *Reportorium Novum*, iii, no. 2 (1963–64).

10 D.D.A.,1845 Parish Report, Murray 31/2.

11 D.D.A.,1848 Parish Report, Murray 32/2.

12 D.D.A., Hamilton Papers, 1834, 35/4, No. 61.

13 D.D.A., Murray Papers, 31/4.

14 D.D.A., Murray Papers, 1835, 31/4.

15 D.D.A., Cullen Papers 1854, 32/2/ 2nd May.

16 P.J. Corish *The Irish Catholic experience* (Dublin, 1985), p. 155

17 D.D.A., Cullen Papers, 1854, 32/2, 2nd May.

18 D.D.A., Cullen Papers, 1863, 340/8, 22nd January.

19 D.D.A., Cullen Papers, 1864, 320/5.

20 D.D.A., McCabe Papers, 1880, 346/2.

21 D.D.A., Cullen Papers, 1871, 335/3.

22 D.D.A., Cullen Papers, 1877, 329/4.

23 Samuel Lewis, *Topographical dictionary of Ireland* (2 vols, London, 1837).

24 D.D.A., Cullen Papers, 1877, 329/4.

25 Green Register of Baptisms, Celbridge R.C. Church.

26 Green Register of Baptisms, Celbridge R.C. Church.

27 D.D.A., Census of the United Parishes of Celbridge and Straffan, 1834, Murray 31/4.

28 *Census of Ireland 1861, pt IV. Reps, Aids and Tables relating to Religious Persuasion, Education and Occupation*, 1863 H.C. (3204–III) lixi, p. 294.

29 *Census of Ireland, Vol. II, Province of Leinster 1872*, H.C. (C.662) lxvii.i, p. 72.

30 R.C.B.L., C.S.V.M. 12/1/1880.

31 D.D.A., Murray Papers, 1842, 33/4.

32 Corish , *The Irish Catholic experience*, p. 203.

33 D.D.A., Murray Papers 1834, Murray 31/4.

34 D.D.A., McCabe Papers, 1880, 346/2.

35 D.D.A., Murray file 33/4 (undated).

36 D.D.A., Cullen Paper 1870, 328/1/1, No. 15.

37 D.D.A., Walsh File, 1892, 23rd January.

38 D.D.A., Hamilton Papers, 1835, 35/5. No. 40.

39 D.D.A., Hamilton Papers, 1835, 35/5. No. 37.

40 D.D.A., Hamilton Papers, 1835, 35/5. No. 42.

41 *Thoms Directory* (Dublin 1865), p. 1171.

42 D.D.A., Cullen Papers 1867, 334/6.

43 Ibid.

44 Ibid.

45 Lena Boylan, 'The Mills of Kildrought', p. 717.

46 *The Royal Commission of Enquiry, Appendix I to Second Report on Education in Ireland, 1805, 1826* (Parochial Abstracts) H.C. 1826027 (12) xii.i, p. 104.

47 *The Catholic Directory,* (Dublin, 1821), Parish of Celbridge.

48 D.D.A., Parish Report, 1833, Murray file 31/4.

49 D.D.A., Census of United Parishes of Celbridge and Straffan, 1834, Murray 31/4.

50 D.D.A., Hamilton Papers, 1834, 35/4, No. 61.

51 D.D.A., 1839 Parish Report, Murray file, 31/7.

52 D.D.A., 1845 Parish Report, Murray file, 31/2.

53 D.D.A., 1848 Parish Report, Murray file, 32/2.

54 D.D.A., Murray Papers, 33/9, No. 26.

55 D.D.A., 1845 Parish Report, Murray 31/2.

56 Corish, *The Irish Catholic experience,* p. 165.

57 National Archive National Board of Education Papers, E.D. 1/43, No. 74.

58 N.A., N.B.E.P., E.D. 1/43, No. 81.

59 N.A., N.B.E.P., E.D. 1/43, No. 8.

60 N.A., N.B.E.P., E.D. 2/146, folio 124–127.

61 N.A., N.B.E.P., E.D. 2/146, folio 124–127.

62 N.A., N.B.E.P., E.D. 2/146, folio 128–129.

63 W.M. Thackary, *The Irish Sketch Book* (London 1879).

64 N.A., Census of Ireland 1901, Parish of Celbridge, 32/14C/1.

65 St. Patrick's Church, Celbridge, Parish Ledger 1855 to 1868.

66 *Rep. Nov.* ii, No. 2, (1960) pp. 395–397.

67 D.D.A., Murray Papers, 1844, 32/1, No. 28.

68 D.D.A., Cullen Papers, 1854, 32/2.

69 Celbridge R.C. Church, Parish Ledger, 1855–1868.

70 'St. Patrick's Church, Celbridge' in *The Irish Builder* i (1859).

71 *Rep. Nov.* ii, No. 2, (1960), pp. 395–397.

72 See handwritten account of Ledger Book written by Fr. John McLoughlin at the centenary of the church in 1959 and now held in Dublin Diocesan Archives.

73 D.D.A, Cullen papers, 1880, 346/2, January 3rd.

74 *Dublin Evening Post,* 7 May, 1842.

75 D.D.A., Cullen Papers 332/6, 1852, No. 9

THE CHURCH OF IRELAND

1 *Census of Ireland 1871, Vol. II, Province of Leinster,* 1872 H.C. (C.662) lxvii.i, p. 95.

2 N.A., Census of Ireland 1901, Parish of Celbridge, 32/14C/1.

3 Donald Harman Akenson, *The Church of Ireland* 1800–1855, (New Haven and London, 1971), p. 337.

4 R.C.B.L., Church of Ireland Celbridge, Collection of Loose Papers.

5 R.C.B.L., C.S.V.M., 9/11/1813.

6 Ibid.

7 Ibid.

8 R.C.B.L., C.S.V.M., 2/5/1882.

9 R.C.B.L., C.S.V.M. 25/2/1883.

10 R.C.B.L., C.S.V.M. 28/7/1884.

11 'Christ Church Celbridge', in *The Irish Builder,* XXVI, No. 594, September 1884.

12 R.C.B.L., J.B. Leslie's Biographical Succession list of the clergy, Parish of Celbridge.

13 D.D.A., Census of the United Parishes of Celbridge and Straffan 1834, Murray file 31/4.

14 Christ Church Celbridge, Parish of Celbridge Preacher's Books (7 vols), 1871–1905.

15 R.C.B.L., C.S.V.M., 25/10/1871.

16 R.C.B.L., C.S.V.M., 4/4/1860.

17 R.C.B.L., C.S.V.M., 25/10/1871.

18 R.C.B.L., C.S.V.M., 17/4/1876.
19 *Slater's Directory of Ireland 1881,* (London and Manchester 1881) pp 380–384.
20 R.C.B.L., C.S.V.M., 4/7/1870.
21 R.C.B.L., C.S.V.M., 20/11/1876.
22 R.C.B.L., C.S.V.M., 1/9/1891.
23 R.C.B.L., C.S.V.M., 30/5/1895.
24 D.D.A., Murray Papers, 31/4, Census of Parish of Celbridge 1834.
25 *Census of Ireland 1861, Pt. IV. Rep. Aids and Table Relating to Religious Persuasion Education and Occupation, 1863,* (3204–111) lix.i. p. 104.
26 *Census of Ireland 1871, Vol. II, Province of Leinster, 1872,* (C.662) lxvii.i, p. 95.
27 Christ Church Celbridge Preacher's Book 1880–1882, 30/6/1881.
28 Christ Church Celbridge Preacher's Book 1888–1894, 30/6/1891.
29 Christ Church Celbridge Preacher's Book 1894–1905, 30/6/1900.
30 Akenson, *The Church of Ireland 1800–1885,* p. 337.
31 R.C.B.L., C.S.V.M., 4/7/1870.
32 R.C.B.L., Celbridge Parish Accounts, Account No. 1 General Sustentation Fund 1872.
33 R.C.B.L., List of Subscribers to General Sustentation Funds 1872–1875, Celbridge Parish Accounts.
34 R.C.B.L., C.S.V.M., 12/1/1880.
35 R.C.B.L., C.S.V.M., 15/8/1881.
36 R.C.B.L., C.S.V.M., 25/2/1883.
37 R.C.B.L., C.S.V.M., 26/7/1890.
38 R.C.B.L., C.S.V.M., 12/4/1887.
39 R.C.B.L., C.S.V.M., 27/6/1887.
40 R.C.B.L., C.S.V.M., 10/3/1891.
41 R.C.B.L., Minute Book of Celbridge Young Mens Christian Association 1862, p.1.
42 D.D.A., Cullen Papers 1854, 32/2, May 2nd.
43 R.C.B.L., Minute Book of Celbridge Y.M.C.A., 16/4/1862, R.C.B.L.
44 R.C.B.L., Minute Book of Celbridge Y.M.C.A., 30/7/1862.
45 R.C.B.L., Minute Book of Celbridge Y.M.C.A., 20/8/1862.
46 R.C.B.L., Minute Book of Celbridge Y.M.C.A., 24/8/1862.
47 R.C.B.L., Minute Book of Celbridge Y.M.C.A., 3/9/1862.
48 R.C.B.L., Minute Book of Celbridge Y.M.C.A., 7/4/1863.
49 R.C.B.L., C.S.V.M, 9/11/1813.
50 Ibid.
51 R.C.B.L., C.S.V.M., 8/6/1824.
52 R.C.B.L., C.S.V.M., 30/4/1830.
53 R.C.B.L., C.S.V.M. 7/4/1827.
54 *A Bill to provide for the composition for Tithes in Ireland* H.C., 1823, (363), ii.
55 R.C.B.L., C.S.V.M., 27/7/1828.
56 R.C.B.L., C.S.V.M. 14/6/1830.
57 R.C.B.L., C.S.V.M. 2/8/1831.
58 R.C.B.L., C.S.V.M. 27/7/1828.
59 R.C.B.L., C.S.V.M., 4/7/1870.
60 Akenson, *The Church of Ireland 1800–1885,* p. 337.
61 R.C.B.L., C.S.V.M., 14/6/1825.
62 *A Bill to put an end to the Establishment of the Church of Ireland and to make provision in respect of the Temporalities thereof, and in respect to the Royal College of Maynooth,* H.C. 1868–69 (27), iii.
63 R.C.B.L., Celbridge Parish Accounts, Introduction to 1871 Accounts.
64 Christ Church Celbridge, Preacher's Book 1880–1882, Visitation Data 30/6/1882.
65 Christ Church Celbridge, Preacher's Book 1894–1905, Visitation Data 30/6/1900.
66 R.C.B.L., C.S.V.M., 1871 to 1882.
67 R.C.B.L., C.S.V.M., 4/7/1870.
68 R.C.B.L., C.S.V.M., 2/5/1882.
69 Christ Church Celbridge, Preacher's Books 1871 to 1905 (7 vols)
70 R.C.B.L., C.S.V.M., 26/7/1890.
71 N.A., N.B.E.P., ED11/43 A, No. 47, 1889.
72 R.C.B.L., C.S.V.M., 1/6/1885
73 *Royal Commission of Enquiry on Education 1826 Ireland, Second Report, Parochial Abstracts,* H.C. 1826–27 (12), xii.i, p. 624.

74 Lena Boylan, 'Thomas Conolly's Kennels', *Celbridge Charter* no. 32, Dec. 1975, Celbridge Library.

75. R.C.B.L., C.S.V.M., 14/4/1866.
76 R.C.B.L., C.S.V.M., 23/4/1878.
77 R.C.B.L., C.S.V.M., 12/1/1880.
78 C.S.V.M., 19/4/1881, R.C.B.L.
79 Akenson, *The Church of Ireland 1800–1885*, p. 202.
80 R.C.B.L., C.S.V.M., 23/6/1889.
81 N.A., National Board of Education Papers, E.C. 9/4912.
82 Ibid.
83 Ibid.
84 N.A., National Board of Education Papers, E.C. 9/4912.
85 Ibid.
86 N.A., National Board of Education Papers, ED9, 12082/89.
87 N.A., National Board of Education Papers, ED9, 12082/89.
88 Christ Church Celbridge, Preacher's Book, 1888–1894,Visitation Data, 30/6/1891.
89 Christ Church Celbridge, Preacher's Book, 1894–1905,Visitation Data, 30/6/1900.
90 T.C.D., Incorporated Society Archives [hereafter I.S.A.], Celbridge Charter School, MS. 5841.
91 Ibid.
92 T.C.D., I.S.A., Celbridge Charter School, MS 5611.
93 *Royal Commission of Enquiry on Education, 1826 Ireland, Second Report, Parochial Abstracts*, H.C. 1826–27 (12), xii.i, p. 624.
94 T.C.D., I.S.A., Celbridge Charter School, MS. 5611.
95 Ibid.
96 T.C.D., I.S.A., Celbridge Charter School, MS. 5841.
97 T.C.D., I.S.A., Celbridge Charter School, school orders, MS. 5612.
98 T.C.D., I.S.A., Celbridge Charter School, MS. 5612, school orders 27/1/1826.
99 T.C.D., I.S.A., Celbridge Charter School, MS. 5612, school orders 6/12/1848.

100 T.C.D., I.S.A., Celbridge Charter School, MS. 5612, school orders 7/11/1849.
101 T.C.D., I.S.A., Celbridge Charter School, MS. 5841, letter dated 2/10/1887.
102 T.C.D., I.S.A., Celbridge Charter School, MS. 5841.
103 R.C.B.L., C.S.V.M., analysis of 1847 Receipts
104 R.C.B.L., Celbridge Poor Accounts 1846 to 1860.
105 R.C.B.L., Celbridge Poor Accounts, January 1855.
106 R.C.B.L., Celbridge Poor Accounts, 29/4/1859.
107 R.C.B.L., Celbridge Poor Accounts, January 1855.
108 R.C.B.L., Celbridge Holy Communion Books, October 1848.
109 R.C.B.L., Celbridge Holy Communion Books, 1846 to 1860.
110 N.A. *Relief Committee, Abstract of Correspondence*, Co. Kildare, 1A/50/83, 15 Nov. 1845.
111 N.A., *1901 Census of Ireland*, Parish of Celbridge, 32/14C.1.

CO-OPERATION AND CONFLICT

1 D.D.A., Catholic Parish Report, 1833, Murray file 31/4.
2 Lena Boylan, 'Lady Louisa's school of Industry', *Celbridge Charter*, No. 32, December 1975, Celbridge Library.
3 Lena Boylan, 'Lady Louisa's school of Industry', *Celbridge Charter*, no. 33, January 1976.
4 Ibid.
5 Ibid.
6 *The Royal Commission on Education, Second Report* 1826, (Parochial Abstracts), H.C. 1826–27 (122) xii.i, page 104.
7 Celbridge R.C. Church Parish Ledger, 1855–1868.

8 R.C.B.L., Celbridge Poor Accounts 1846–1860.

9 D.D.A., Catholic Parish Report 1820, Murray file 31/2, no. 1362.

10 D.D.A., Census of the United Parishes of Celbridge and Straffan, 1834, Murray 31/4.

11 D.D.A., Murray file 35/4, No. 61, 1834.

12 Ibid.

13 D.D.A., Murray file 32/1, No. 28, 1844.

14 D.D.A., Cullen Papers 1854, 32/2, No. 192.

15 D.D.A., Cullen Papers May 1854, 32/2.

16 Ibid.

17 Ibid.

18 Ibid.

19 R.C.B.L., C.S.V.M, 25/8/1884.

20 R.C.B.L., C.S.V.M., 3/3/1893.

21 D.D.A., Cullen papers, file 340/1, May 1861.

22 *Dublin Evening Mail*, 28 May 1861.

23 Ibid.

24 D.D.A., Cullen file 1861, May 3rd, No. 21.

25 *Dublin Evening Mail*, 31 May 1861.

26 Ibid.

27 Ibid.

28 Ibid.

29 Ibid.

30 *Dublin Evening Mail*, 3 June 1861.

31 Ibid.

32 Ibid.

33 D.D.A., Cullen papers 1861, June 6th.

34 Ibid.

35 *Dublin Evening Mail*, 4 June, 1861.

36 Ibid.

37 Ibid.

38 Engraving on base of Celtic cross which stands outside entrance door of Roman Catholic Church, Main Street, Celbridge.

39 *Thom's Irish Almanac and Official Directory 1863*, (Dublin, 1863), p. 1105.